Praise for Julia Cook and *Teach Kids, Not Content*

"*Teach Kids, Not Content* is a must read for all K–12 educators. Every aspect teaching and classroom life is presented in a realistic and doable manner. The author's words are driven by a key ingredient of effective teaching—relationship building! Each highly readable chapter provides techniques and strategies that build connections with students. Written from classroom experience, *Teach Kids, Not Content* is an authentic difference maker for educators at any stage of their professional career."

**–Dr. Mary Jo Melvin, Professor of Education,
Pennsylvania Western University**

"This timely book engages the reader to face important truths about teaching children. Julia Cook shares her experiences and heartfelt classroom stories alongside insightful step-by-step strategies. *Teach Kids, Not Content* showcases her love for children and how much she values their perspective. Julia encourages us to lead with our hearts when it comes to developing the minds of children."

–Bridget Barnes, Director, Common Sense Parenting

"*Teach Kids, Not Content* highlights the importance of authentic connection and offers a call to each of us as educators to remember the 'why' that first brought us into this profession. Through stories and anecdotes, this book offers hope, humor, and a reminder of how, even in the smallest of moments, we can make a difference in the lives of our young students."

–Sarah I. Springer, PhD, LPC, ACS

"As a teacher, principal, and district administrator for 30 years, I highly recommend *Teach Kids, Not Content* to reinvigorate school staff. The book is practical and can bring value to individual teachers, book studies, and in professional development."

**–Christine Garbe, Owner and CEO,
Fireweed Educational Consulting**

TEACH KIDS, NOT CONTENT

TEACH KIDS, NOT CONTENT

HOW TO CONNECT WITH STUDENTS AND LOVE TEACHING AGAIN

Julia Cook

JOSSEY-BASS™
A Wiley Brand

Contents

Preface

I am a firm believer in the phrase: *"You can't TALK THE TALK if you haven't WALKED THE WALK!"* As a former middle school teacher and school counselor, I have been given the opportunity to authentically walk in your shoes.

My career in education started years ago with a conversation between me and my father.

> "Juli, you've been in college for six years! You need to get your degree and graduate! I'm tired of paying tuition! What are you plans?"
>
> "I don't really have a plan. I have no idea what I want to be!"
>
> "What do you love doing?"
>
> "I love teaching kids how to ski!"
>
> "Well then get a teaching certificate and teach school!"
>
> "Teach school? Are you serious?"
>
> "Kids learn to ski by seeing what to do and then trying it. If you can teach kids how to ski, you can teach anything!"

. . . So that's what I did! I became a teacher!!!!!

I was an inner-city middle school math teacher. I loved my job, and I loved my kids, but it seemed like I had to stand on my head and pick my nose to get my 9th graders to pay attention – and this was before the onset of social media. Getting street-smart geniuses to care about and even relate to the importance of learning algebra was a tall order. Attendance was a huge issue, so I first had to find a way to make coming to my class more inviting and valuable. What we did every day had to be more meaningful to my students than skipping.

I had to see the world through their eyes, learn to appreciate their challenges, and validate their worth.

It was exhausting, and at times I felt hopeless and highly ineffective. Not to mention the fact that I had little kids of my own and a husband who also needed support and deserved a wife.

It didn't take me long to realize that if I wanted to survive at school, I needed to pick my battles. One morning, I walked outside of my house to find my car vandalized and my husband's newly installed stereo system gone. That morning at work, I must have been wearing a defeated expression, because one of my kids asked, "What's wrong?"

"Somebody broke into my car and stole my husband's brand-new stereo. We just had it installed two weeks ago."

"What kind of car you got, Cook?" one of my boys asked.

"A red Chevy Chevette." ·

The squelched look on that boy's face said it all as I heard him say under his breath, "Uh Oh!" I knew it was him . . . and he knew I knew it was him.

I could have called the police, had him arrested, and lost him for the entire rest of the semester. But he was worth more to me than a stereo. At the end of class, I walked over to that boy and said, "I want it put back in, and I want it done right!"

The next morning when I opened my car door, the stereo had been neatly reinstalled, and the minor damages to the dashboard were quite skillfully repaired. No words were ever spoken about that event again, but that day, a connection of unconditional positive regard was established between us, and that boy knew that I had his back . . . and he had mine.

My school district at that time was continually pushing everyone toward graduate education hours. They were also offering access to a government program that would help cover tuition, so I figured a degree in school counseling might help me become a better teacher. My plan was to never leave the classroom, but when we moved to Fremont, Nebraska, and their school district was merging four elementary schools into one big building, they were in high need of a school counselor. I decided to apply.

Hmmm! Surprise . . . I found out that I LOVED school counseling too!

About two years into my school counseling career, my kids were really struggling with tattling – schoolwide. The teachers were about ready to pull out their hair! "We need you to do a lesson on tattling!" they said. "And we need it *now*!"

During graduate school, I had an amazing instructor, Anita Theophilus, who taught me that if you really want to get into a child's head, you read them a story. If the story has great people skills woven into it, and the kids can relate to the characters, they will naturally absorb those skills into their worldview and practice applying them. Bibliotherapy became my jam!

I looked feverishly for a book on tattling, and I could not find one that said what I wanted my kids to hear, so I wrote my ideas down, came up with a storyline, and illustrated the plot with coloring book pictures. Keep in mind this was way before GOOGLE IMAGES!

I tried out the story with my students and it worked! Fast forward 20 years, and there are now over 100 Julia Cook titles in print, in nine languages.

The books are used all over the world, and nearly 4 million copies have been sold. However, none of it would have happened if kids didn't see themselves in the book pages; if the teachers, counselors, therapists, and parents didn't see value in the content; and if my amazing publishers didn't believe in me. For that, I thank you all from the bottom of my heart.

In September 2024, I launched a resource website (`cookiebytesby julia.com`) that includes audiobooks of every title, grab-and-go activities, and concrete visual ideas. I was contacted shortly after by Jossey-Bass – Wiley Publishing, asking me to write this book for educators. Straying from my genre comfort zone has been a unique challenge, but the experiences I have gained through this process have helped me grow in ways I never thought possible.

With this book, my hope is to offer you the same kind of practical, heart-driven tools that have guided me throughout my career – tools that help you connect, inspire, and make a difference every day.

BEST!

Julia

Introduction

Are you an educator or an aspiring teacher in the making? Are you feeling overwhelmed, worn out, or discouraged?

Does it seem like the energy in your classroom is working against you? Do you drive home every afternoon (or evening) feeling that you're not enough?

Are you wondering where your "difference-making joy" has gone? Is your job *not* what you signed up to do?

If you answered yes to any or all of these questions, this book is for you.

Teach Kids, Not Content will give you authentic insight into the challenges that come along with teaching today's kids and ignite ideas that will help you tackle those challenges more effectively. I have identified key concepts that can help everyone who works with kids become better at what they do.

These areas of focus make up the chapters of this book and are packed full of heartfelt stories, real-life experiences, and practical tips and tools. The most important part of this book, however, is to serve as a reminder of why you chose to go into teaching and authenticate your worth!

The purpose of this book is to convey three things to everyone who chooses to read it:

- To effectively teach children, you must enter their view of the world!
- The content we are teaching can never be more important than the kids we are teaching it to.
- Every behavior (or misbehavior) is a result of an unmet need.
- When it comes to effective teaching, the relationships that you build with your students heavily outweigh the subject knowledge that you possess.

This book presents overall concepts of these three components through personal stories, meaningful experiences, and authentic examples.

Christa McAuliffe – an astronaut and teacher who died tragically in the 1986 Challenger space shuttle explosion once said, *"I touch the future. I teach."* You make a profound impact on your students, and you play a huge role in shaping our future by doing what you do every single day.

Kids need us now more than ever! If reading this book can help future educators become more effective and keep even just one talented teacher from leaving our profession, that's a win!

Teach Kids, Not Content

"Every child deserves a champion – an adult who will never give up on them, who understands the power of connection and insists that they become the best that they can possibly be."

–*Rita Pierson*

Mrs. Hansen asked all of us to sit on the reading rug. She sat down in front on the floor. "Come in close," she said. We all scooted up. Mrs. Hansen leaned in. I can still picture her face that day . . . tears fighting hard to avoid rolling down her cheeks.

"Today is your very last day as a kindergartener at Franklin School. When you come back from summer break, you will all be first graders!" I remember how cool that sounded. I was finally going to get to be a "grader."

"It's also your last day with me as your teacher, and I have taught you everything I can think of."

"It's very important to always remember that *you* will always be one of Mrs. Hansen's kids. I believe in you, and you will all live in my heart forever!"

"Today, I am going to give every one of you a very special gift . . . It's a key to my heart."

Mrs. Hansen took the lid off a fancy gift-wrapped box, and inside were old worn-out keys tied to beautiful silky ribbons. She handed out the key necklaces, and asked us to put them on.

"Now grab onto your key and look at me. If ever you find yourself in a tricky situation and you feel like there is a door in front of you that you can't open, squeeze your key with your thumb and your finger, close your eyes, take a deep breath, and remember . . . I am one of Mrs. Hansen's kids and she believes in me! I can figure this out! I can do it! Your special key will remind you to believe in yourself. It will help you open any door that is in your way."

(Continued)

That was 55 years ago, and I still have the key to Mrs. Hansen's heart.
I often tell this story and hold up my key, tattered ribbon and all, when I speak to educators. Many of you went into this field because you had a teacher like Mrs. Hansen.

A teacher who showed you how to believe in yourself.

A teacher who saw your gifts, encouraged you to share them, and rewarded you with appreciation for doing so.

A teacher who made a positive difference in your life.

Now it's your turn. Now YOU are supposed to be the difference maker.

Breaking Out of Survival Mode

The reality is that teaching is one of the most important professions on the planet, yet it can also be one of the most challenging. You're faced with repeated demands for expected test performance, overloaded content amount with limited delivery time, minimal financial resources for creative teaching materials, large classroom sizes, and behavior challenges up the wazoo! Some of the systems currently in place don't appear to be effective. And to top it all off, there's a huge lack of authentic understanding of the obstacles that you are expected to overcome.

As a result of all this, you may feel overworked and undervalued.

Instead of focusing on your students, you are catapulted into survival mode. What was supposed to be rewarding, doable, and fun at times seems impossible and overwhelming.

So why do you do it? Possibly because you had a teacher like Mrs. Hansen who helped you realize your internal worth and taught you firsthand the importance of sharing it. Maybe because you believe first and foremost in helping the kids. I often say, "If you don't enjoy teaching, you might be working too hard in the wrong direction. If you can figure out how to redirect the energy in your classroom and make it work for you instead of against you, you'll get your joy back!"

Remember: The Kids Are Still Kids

Being "in the trenches" daily for nearly a quarter of a century, and experiencing kid interactions both pre-and post-COVID, has taught me a lot.

I often hear people say, "Kids have changed!" I disagree with parts of this statement. The immediate situations surrounding our children have indeed changed drastically over time, and will continue to change, but kids are still kids.

Child behaviors have evolved as a result of the new experiences, but again – *kids are still kids*. They will push button A to make B happen. If that doesn't work, they'll try pushing C, D, R, Y, and any other button they can reach to meet their basic needs.

SEE ME, HEAR ME, and VALIDATE ME.

It's important to always keep in mind that every student misbehavior you encounter results from an unmet need.

In this post-pandemic time, we all want to blame COVID.

The COVID-19 pandemic disrupted learning, challenged engagement, and reduced instructional time. According to the World Health Organization, the prevalence of anxiety and depression increased in both children and adults globally by 25%. Approximately 37% of US high school students reported experiencing poor mental health during the pandemic. This was most likely a result of shifting to remote learning which caused kids to feel increasingly isolated, home-bound, tied to technology, and sedentary – all factors which contribute to increased anxiety and depression.[1]

---

[1] Annie E. Casey Foundation, "Impact of Covid-19 on Mental Health," The Annie E. Casey Foundation website, February 21, 2025, https://www.aecf.org/blog/impact-of-covid-19-on-mental-health.

So, yes, we all are desperately playing catch-up. I know firsthand when speaking to kids post-pandemic, I have to use 8× the amount of energy to keep my audience engaged and on target. It can be exhausting!

COVID can be one reason for why teaching has become more difficult–but we cannot continue to allow it to be an excuse for not untapping potential in our kids.

Engaging to Hold Their Attention

During my first year of teaching, I stood up in front of 38 middle schoolers to give what I thought would be an amazing lesson on the distributive property. This was my annual observation, and both my vice principal and principal were in the back of the room ready to watch.

I was so excited! I'd spent days memorizing the textbook examples, formatting my introduction and planning out my objectives. I loved teaching math, and I couldn't wait to show my admin what I could do.

This was going to be my *jam lesson*!

I started off with what I thought would be a creative and original bang, explaining the history and origin of how the distributive property came about. Then, I continued by perfectly regurgitating the examples from the textbook.

My lesson went from bad to worse.

It started off like a slow, leaking flat tire, and quickly spun itself into a shredded blowout.

We're talking *total bust*!

The more I talked and tried to explain the content, the less engaged and more out of touch my kids became. I wasn't connecting with any of them at all!

When I looked up and saw the expression of hopeless disappointment on my VP's chalky white face, my heart started pounding and my head started to spin. My principal was voraciously writing a novel of notes. "He's probably gathering any and all evidence he needs to terminate me," I thought. My anxiety went thru the roof, and a firestorm of bad thoughts rushed through my head.

I'm going to lose my job!

Why did I ever think I could be good at this?

How can I support my family with my husband in school full time if they don't renew my contract?

I don't feel safe here.

I want to go home right now.

I need to hug my kids.

And then, it hit me . . . right in the face like an ice-cold water balloon.

This morning before I left home, I hugged each one of my kids individually and distributed my love evenly to them.

That's it!

My students don't care about math theory, *but they do care about hugs*!

"OK, this lesson is obviously not going well. Let's try something different," I said. I slid my arm across my teaching table and everything that was on it crashed onto the floor, shocking everyone. Then I sat on top of the table.

My VP's mouth dropped open with concerned surprise and my principal's pen fell to the floor as he stood up out of his chair. (I bet they thought I was really losing it.)

"We all make mistakes and today with this lesson, I made a big one. I tried to teach you all about the distributive property the wrong way. I need you to give me a DO-OVER. Forget about everything I've told you so far and with your permission, I'd like to start over."

My kids looked at me like I was from outer space, but at least I had everyone's full attention.

I wrote this on the board:

$$ME(Carson + Gates + Courtney)$$

"You all know that I have three kids. Every morning before I come to school, I hug each one of them individually, so they know how much I love them. I 'DISTRIBUTE' my love between the three of my kids equally, because if I only hugged one of them, the other two would get jealous. Like this:"

$$ME(Carson) + ME(Gates) + ME(Courtney)$$

"That's just like the DISTRIBUTIVE PROPERTY in math."

Then I wrote this equation on the board:

$$7(a + b + c)$$

"Seven is the mom and a, b, and c are her kids. If she wants her kids to be happy, she needs to distribute her love evenly and hug each one of them which looks like this:"

$$7a + 7b + 7c$$

My students immediately became engaged. They understood my story and all of the sudden, the distributive property started to make sense to them. We spent the rest of the period doing example problems as a group, and everyone was smiling at the end, including me!

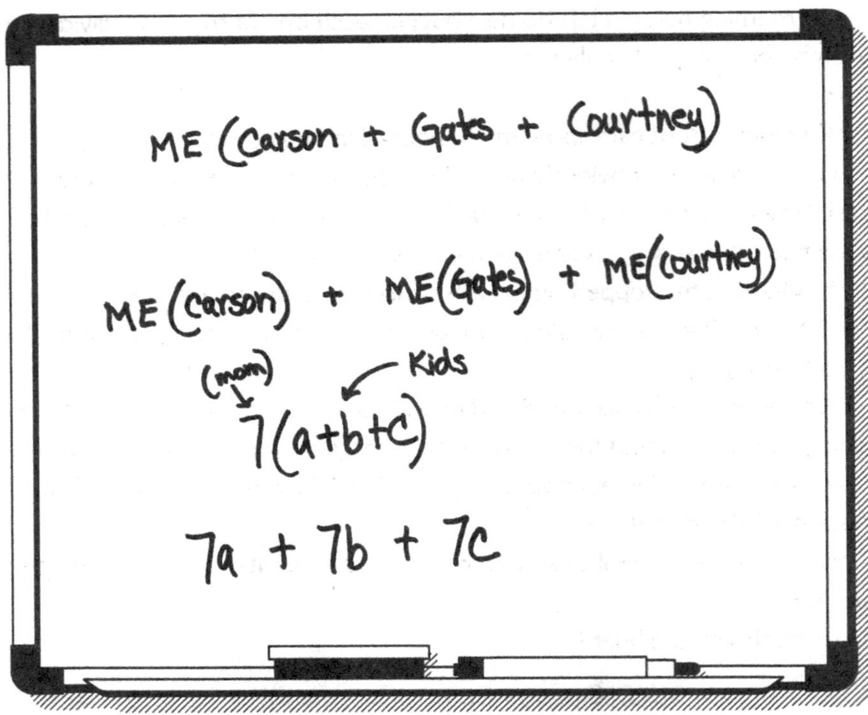

"I'm not a math person at all. In fact, I hated math as a kid," my VP said after class. "But today, I learned something that I will never forget, and you made it fun. Well done!"

"Was this staged?" my principal asked me. "Did you start off doing poorly on purpose so your students would realize that everyone makes mistakes, even teachers?"

"Uh, yep! How'd I do?"

"It was an amazing lesson with two important messages. You did awesome!"

Whew! – a true bullet dodged.

I still feel a bit guilty lying to my boss, but boy did I learn big that day!

If you want to teach something to a kid and make it stick, find a way to relate your content to their view of the world.

Thanks to the use of technology, students today are inundated with information at their fingertips, and accessing it is almost effortless. However, convincing a child that the content you are teaching them is valuable and worth being internalized is a true art form.

For kids to effectively learn, they first must be willing to pay attention long enough to let new information enter their heads.

Then, they need to figure out ways to relate that information to *their own personal view of the world* by:

- Seeing it
- Hearing it
- Feeling it
- Doing it
- Demonstrating it to somebody else
- (And most important of all) Relating it to something they already know.

This learning process creates a tall order for teachers, but the payoff is immeasurable.

Building Relationships

Most students have two questions rolling around in their heads every time they step foot inside your classroom:

"Why should I do _____?"

and

"When I do _____, what do I get?" AKA "What's in it for me?"

As shown and shared by Yale child psychologist James Comer, Missouri educator Justin Tarte, New Zealand academic John Hattie, and others, teaching success and effectiveness depends heavily on the relationships that you build with your students, and less upon how much subject knowledge you have.

You can be the most knowledgeable educator on the planet, but if your students can't see worth in your words, they won't make the effort to listen to what you are saying.

Think about it . . . Would you want to pay attention to someone you couldn't relate to or somebody you didn't like? If kids feel *seen*, *heard*, and *validated* when they are around you, they will want to stay in your classroom because YOU are meeting their basic needs!

If the "what" you are teaching holds a bigger place in your heart than the "who" you are teaching it to, the energy in your room will funnel against you, and your students will do whatever it takes to find ways to leave.

I found this out the hard way one year . . .

It was only week three with the most challenging group of 7th grade math students I had ever taught. I thought I was pretty good at making connections with kids, and making math relatable and fun, but with this group, I found myself at a loss. Was I losing my touch? The class was overall pretty good, but one climate-changer in this group ate my joy for lunch on a daily basis and then threw it up in my face!

TJ talked when I talked, revolutionized class clowning, mastered the art of unkind eye rolling, and sucked up every molecule of oxygen in the room.

He had absolutely no interest in listening to anything I had to say. He just wanted everyone's undivided attention. When he was absent, my class was great, but every time he walked through my door, a dark cloud of "whatever" followed overhead. He made my 3rd-period class 49 minutes of living hell.

The easy thing to do would have been to kick TJ out of class.

That's what most teachers did.

But the last thing this kid needed was more detention and/or suspension. I had to do something, because TJ's dark cloud was unleashing an energetic torrential rainstorm on a daily basis, and I was drowning!

One day, I borrowed a student teacher and asked her to sit in on my class. As soon as TJ's cloud started to rain, I grabbed my backpack, emptied it out on my desk, and walked over by him.

"TJ, I whispered. Let's go on a walk,"

"You kickin' me out?" he asked.

"Not on your life! I need to take a walk, and I want you to go with me. Let's go!"

I walked outside through the front door and TJ followed.

We walked across the street and stood on the sidewalk next to a city owned, curb-lined rock garden. "You seem to be carrying around a lot of stuff," I said.

He looked at me with a questioning face. Then he tilted his head slightly and gave me a side eye: *Are you for real?*

I took his skepticism in stride.

"I have no idea what's going on in your life, TJ, but I can only imagine how hard things are for you. Can you trust me enough to try something?"

"I guess," he said, hesitantly.

"See this empty backpack? See these rocks? For everything that's bugging you today, I want you to pick up a rock, tell me what that rock stands for, and then put it in this backpack."

TJ shrugged his shoulders, reached for the backpack, and started grabbing rocks.

"My mom died last year. She did drugs. We couldn't find her. The snow plow guy found her when he moved a bunch of snow.

"My dad's in prison. He's a druggie.

"I live with my grandma in her car. She's too poor for a house.

"The judge makes me go to school and I hate it."

My eyes filled with tears as he continued . . .

"I don't have any friends," TJ said. "I'm starving. My brother was in a gang – but he got shot . . . I miss him."

Here stood this kid with a backpack full of rocks that was so heavy, Superman would have a tough time lifting it.

No wonder he doesn't care about math!

When TJ finished, I zipped the backpack shut and had him put it on. Together, we slowly walked up to the front door of the school.

"I am so amazed by you, TJ. That's a lot to haul around, and you do it every single day! You are a really strong kid."

As I grabbed the door handle I said, "OK, I want you to take off the backpack and set it outside of this door and then walk inside."

He did it, and I continued.

"TJ, hard things in our lives weigh us down like a backpack full of rocks. But did you know that when you enter this building, you can leave your rocks outside by the door before you come in? You don't have to bring them in with you. Inside this school, and especially inside my classroom, you can just be a kid. Your rocks will be there waiting for you when you leave, but when you're here, you can just be TJ."

Then I grabbed a couple of granola bars out of the staff room.

"Eat these on the way back up to my room, and let's start today over."

After that, TJ was a different kid. He started to add to my class, as opposed to take from it. He still had his storms, and when he did, I would point to my backpack and he would ask to leave my room for a restroom break, and then reenter a few minutes later, *backpackless*.

Once TJ realized that he was more important to me than math, a human connection was made and a positive relationship flourished.

TJ felt seen, heard, and validated.

Instead of doing everything in his power to get kicked out of my class, he tried his best to stay in there. And it didn't take him long to discover that he was really good at math.

Your students are, and always will be, more important than anything you teach them.

From "Teaching" to "Learning"

In his book, *Activating the Desire to Learn*, Bob Sullo writes about a social studies teacher whose goals went from "covering" all the material, to then "teaching" the material to finally shifting her emphasis to her students "learning" the material, even if she covered less.

This teacher shifted the focus from her "teaching" to the students "learning."[2]

If you make the mistake of valuing your content over your kids, you'll drown.

To me, being a teacher is kinda like being a vacuum cleaner. Your power to be effective is based on the relationships you build with your students. You can be the best vacuum cleaner ever invented, and push yourself across the floor all day long . . . but without power, your effort becomes wasted energy, and you can't draw anyone in.

Instead of *teaching "great stuff" to our kids*, we need to refrain and start *teaching our kids "great stuff!"*

---

[2]Sullo, Bob, *Activating the Desire to Learn*, Association for Supervision and Curriculum Development (ASCD), Alexandria, VA, 2007, p. 79.

Worth Remembering

- If you don't enjoy your job as a teacher, you may be working too hard in the wrong direction. If you can figure out how to redirect the energy in your classroom and make it work for you as opposed to against you, you'll get your joy back!
- Typical teaching challenges include: repeated demands for expected test performance, overloaded content amount with limited delivery time, minimal financial resources for creative teaching materials, large classroom sizes, and numerous behavior challenges.
- Many people lack an authentic understanding of the obstacles teachers are expected to overcome.
- The COVID-19 epidemic heavily challenged student and teacher engagement, dramatically reduced instructional time, squelched student understanding, and made teaching even more difficult.
- COVID-19 can indeed be a reason for why things have changed, but it cannot continue to be an excuse for untapping potential in our kids.
- Every misbehavior is a result of an unmet need.
- Every child needs three things: To be *seen*. To be *heard*. To be *validated*.
- In order for today's kids to effectively learn new content, they first must be willing to:
  - Pay attention long enough to let the information enter their heads.
  - Figure out ways to relate that information to their own personal view of the world by seeing it, hearing it, feeling it, doing it, demonstrating it to somebody else, and most importantly, relating it to something they already know.
- Most kids have two questions every time they enter your classroom: "Why should I do _______?" and "When I do_______, what do I get?" AKA: "What's in it for me?"
- Teaching success and effectiveness depends heavily on the relationships that you build with your students, and less upon how much knowledge you have.
- Your students are, and always will be, more important than anything you teach them.

Instead of teaching content to your students . . . teach your students content. Kids come first. Content comes second. If you lead with heart, the learning will follow.

Worth Trying

- At the beginning of each day, or at the beginning of each class period, let your students unload and or share what is going on in their lives before you start to teach. This authentically shows your kids that you are putting who they are above what you want them to learn, gives you more effective insight on your teaching audience, and allows them to free up brain space and reduce anxiety.

- Littles – HIGH, LOW, AND SPRINKLE! (5–10 minutes)
- Take turns (you included) sharing your:
  - HIGH – The best thing that happened to you since the last time we met.
  - LOW – The worst thing that happened to you since the last time we met.
  - SPRINKLE – How you showed kindness or received kindness since the last time we met.
  - Bigs – WHAT'S IN *YOUR* BACKPACK? (10 minutes)
- Read or share parts of TJ's story and explain to your students that hard things weigh us down like a backpack full of rocks. Download the "What's In *Your* Backpack" activity sheet from the *Kids Before Content* section at the Cookie-bytes website or make copies of the illustration of TJ's backpack and allow kids to label the rocks with the things that are weighing them down.

02 I Need a Large Recharge! – Building Mental Wellness

"A fire hydrant that runs out of water cannot do its job . . . even if it has a perfect connection with a hose that reaches."

-Julia Cook

Teaching is a GIVE, GIVE, GIVE profession . . . have you noticed?

And our students seem to find a way to TAKE, TAKE, TAKE.

Students today face a truly unique combination of ongoing struggles. From behavioral problems, diversity issues, multiple levels of inequities (socioeconomic, physical, emotional, social, athletic, academic, etc.) to increasing mental health challenges, suicidal ideation, career focus stress, and community health concerns, there's a lot going on in their young lives. Sprinkle in the influence of social media, and it's like pouring gas directly onto the struggle fire.

Ironically, we too are facing many of these same issues ourselves.

As a result, many teachers leave their buildings on a daily basis thinking, "I am NOT enough!"

Reality starts to take a toll on our mental wellness, and our difference-making magic feels like it's being sucked down a drain. If this is you, and you feel like you are burning out, you are not alone.

The **Pew Research Center** asked 2,500 teachers for their view and experiences on a wide range of issues. Teachers stated chronic absenteeism, poverty, anxiety, and depression are the most serious problems affecting their schools.[1] They also reported not having enough time in the day to do their jobs properly.

(Continued)

---

[1]Braga, Dana, Kiley Hurst, Shannon Greenwood, Nick Zanetti, and John Carlo Mandapat, "What Public K-12 Teachers Want Americans to Know About Teaching," Pew Research Center, April 4, 2024, https://www.pewresearch.org/social-trends/2024/04/04/what-public-k-12-teachers-want-americans-to-know-about-teaching/.

When asked why, they said performing nonteaching duties (hallway monitoring, lunch room duty, recess supervision, etc.) helping kids outside of classroom time, and covering for other teachers when they are not available are the main contributors.

They also noted that as a teacher, it is extremely difficult to achieve a healthy work–life balance.

> "Teachers serve multiple roles other than being responsible for teaching curriculum. We are counselors, behavioral specialists, and parents for students who need us to fill those roles. We sacrifice a lot to give all of ourselves to the role as a teacher."
> *–Elementary School Teacher." – Pew Research Center Survey*[2]

If you're getting tired of circling the drain, and it's causing you to lose your effectiveness in the classroom, you owe it to yourself and your students to PLUG UP THAT DRAIN and find a way to RECHARGE what you have left so you can figure out how to REPLACE what you have lost.

Think about it this way.

Every time you board a plane, a flight attendant says, "If oxygen masks are needed, be sure you secure your own mask first before assisting others."

This is truly great advice.

Think about it . . . If you pass out, how are you going to help anyone else?

Plug That Drain

Take out a sheet of paper and write down anything and everything that's currently stressing you out – work, home, family issues, friend issues, financial issues . . . everything. Don't hold back. Unzip your brain and metaphorically pour those stressors right onto the page.

Grab a second sheet of paper and draw a saucer-sized circle in the center. Now, look at your list. If you personally have control over a stressor on your list, write it down inside the circle. If the stressor is out of your control, write it down outside of the circle. When you are finished, take notice.

All of your stressors are represented and validated.

---

[2]Ibid.

Now make a conscious effort to use your energy and your other valuable resources wisely. Focus on only those stressors you can control. . . . In a nut-shell . . . STAY IN YOUR HULA HOOP!

Thank you Stephen Convey for introducing us to the Circle of Influence®.[3]

Recharge

One Thursday after doing a full-day presentation at an elementary, I was invited to sit in on a whole staff faculty meeting after school. The principal asked me to take about 10 minutes at the end of the meeting and highlight some of the strate-gies I use while presenting.

"This is going to be fun – *not!*" I thought. I was toast after a full day, and I could only imagine how tired the teachers were.

Sure enough, I saw an array of numerous worn-out looking faces as the teachers entered the room.

"Yep, I know how you feel . . . I've been there," I thought to myself.

But, as the teachers sat down, their emotions seemed to lighten up a bit.

Surprisingly, their eyes started to smile, and the affect in the room went from flat to curvy fun.

On the table in front of each chair sat three blank postcards and a 5 × 8 piece of cardstock. In the center of each table was a kid-decorated soup can, filled with markers and multicolored gel pens, a pile of fun stickers, and of course a pile of candy (including chocolate) for the teachers to munch on.

The principal began passing out slightly picked-over sheets of peel-and-stick labels. It didn't take me long to realize the labels were printed with the names and addresses of the students in each teacher's class. Stressed faces cracked smiles as the teachers looked over the names, chose three labels from their sheets, stuck them to the back of the postcards and started writing.

"What are they doing?" I asked the principal.

"At the beginning of every faculty meeting, each teacher writes a positive postcard to three of their students. Then I mail them out the next day. Throughout the school year, every kid receives a fun postcard in the mail hand written by their teacher. The students get recognized and feel more valued and appreciated when they see it in print, and my teachers start each faculty meeting with a posi-tive mindset."

---

[3]Covey, Stephen R., *The 7 Habits of Highly Effective People: Restoring the Character Ethic* [Rev. ed.], Free Press, 2004, p. 83.

"What is the 5 × 8 card for?"

"Giving positives is huge, but getting them is even bigger. On this card, they write an 'I appreciate you because . . .' note to another staff member. Then we read these out loud before we leave. Faculty meetings are not fun for anyone, so I like to start with a positive and end on a positive. Then the middle stuff isn't so hard to sit through. It really helps with teacher morale."

You can find positives and negatives in every human experience. Making a conscious choice to recognize, internalize, and celebrate the positives will provide the fuel you need to recharge and rebuild your soul, making your internal light brighter. Living in the negative, on the other hand, will hastily consume the fuel you have left in the tank until you burn out.

Replace

A mentally well person can be defined as someone who is resilient, hopeful, has a positive outlook on life, is able to solve problems, is capable of managing emotions effectively, is involved in meaningful relationships, and stays joyfully active. When stress depletes our mental well-being, it's important to replace what we have lost.

The *World Health Organization* says the definition of mental wellness is living in a state of well-being in which people realize their own abilities, are capable of coping with the stresses of life, can work productively and fruitfully, and can make contributions to their community.[4]

Building our mental wellness and replenishing what we lose from the daily struggles we face is not easy, but it is doable. According to the *New Economics Foundation*, there are five things you can do to build your mental wellness:[5]

- Connect
- Take Notice
- Move
- Keep Learning
- Give

---

[4]WHO Staff, "Mental Health," June 17, 2022, https://www.who.int/news-room/fact-sheets/detail/mental-health-strengthening-our-response.

[5]Stevens, Lucie, "Five Ways to Wellbeing at a Time of Social Distancing," New Economics Foundation, March 30, 2020, https://neweconomics.org/2020/03/five-ways-to-wellbeing-at-a-time-of-social-distancing.

It takes all five to do it right, but the combination of how much of each is as individualized as a fingerprint.

Just like with the oxygen mask, once you've helped yourself, you can pass on these same five techniques to your students.

When you win, they win!

The trick however, to making all of this work effectively, is to recognize the importance of small steps along the way. The little things you do for yourself every day really add up! On the flip side, if you space your ladder rungs too far apart by trying to do more than you are possibly capable of, climbing the ladder of mental wellness becomes discouraging, out of reach, and self-defeating.

Connect with Others – Outside the Classroom

One very early morning, while flying out of my hometown airport, I noticed a woman in front of me was having a tough time getting her carry-on luggage up on the screening belt. When the TSA agent gave her a hand, she turned around and I could tell immediately by the unsure look in her eyes this lady was not used to traveling.

The minute she walked through the scanners, her artificial hip set the alarms off in every direction. I watched her waver and almost lose her balance in an attempt to keep an eye on her luggage as she was getting a full-body massage by TSA. The look of discomfort on her face doubled by the second.

I decided to stand in front of her luggage on the belt until she got done so I could help her take it off.

"Here, let me help you with your bags," I said.

She thanked me, and I immediately noticed a tear streaming down her cheek. I asked if she was okay.

"No," she answered as she attempted to gather her things.

I helped her over to a bench and we sat down.

"I found out yesterday my daughter has a brain tumor and I'm on my way to take care of her . . . A brain tumor!" she repeated, her eyes flooding with more tears. "I'm supposed to be the strong one. Look at me! How can I be the strong one?"

"Well, you're her mom!" I said. "Moms always know what to say, what to do, and how to help. You are one of the people she needs the most right now. You'll do just fine and you'll find a way to be strong enough, because you are her mom!"

We sat together and chit-chatted for a few minutes until the tears stopped flowing, and I helped her over to the chairs by her gate. She was 3 hours early, and my flight was boarding in 10 minutes. I walked over to the Delta desk to talk with a young agent who I knew quite well. I explained how hard today has been and will be for my newest friend.

"She can't just sit there all by herself for three hours, and I need to board."

"Don't worry, Julia," he said. "I'll keep an eye on her and make sure she's okay. I promise."

As I stepped onto the jet bridge for my flight, I glanced over to her gate, and there was that 24-year-old kid sitting next to my new friend with his arm resting on the back of her chair in case she needed a hug.

My eyes welled up with tears as I walked toward the plane.

Wow! If I hadn't asked the lady if she was okay and taken a genuine minute to listen to her reply, I would have missed out on something priceless . . . helping.

I really grew that day. I felt like I mattered, and I can only imagine how significant the young Delta employee must have felt.

Never be too busy to make connections with others. Speak to somebody new, and say "Hello. How are you?" and then genuinely listen to their response.

Also, encourage your students to do the same by sharing "helping stories" that spread positivity in the classroom.

Everyone needs a human dustpan occasionally. This is especially true if you have a tough job like teaching. A human dustpan is the person who listens as you vent and keeps your conversation safe. Emotional purging is an essential must when maintaining your mental wellness. So, if you don't already have a good human dustpan, find one!

As teachers, we are sometimes fortunate enough to be chosen as human *dustpans* by our students. They vent to us, and we sweep it all up, collecting a wide variety of "stuff," some valuable . . . and some . . . not so much.

It is our job to sort out the precious gems from the rubble, hold on tight to the former, toss out the latter, and simply take in what is given without comment or complaint.

For example, when Freddy gives us an in-depth play-by-play of the latest episode of his favorite TV show, we sweep his words into our dustpan because it's important to him. When Tiera goes on and on (and on . . .) about her cat, we fill our dustpan to the brim and show her a genuine presence by paying attention – even though a part of us could care less.

Being a good *human dustpan* for our students is validating for them. It lets our kids know we genuinely care and are willing to actively listen to what they have to say.

The connections we make with our family, friends, colleagues, and neighbors hold us up in times of need, and help us form the foundation of who we are.

Take Notice of What's Going On Around You

"You need to be more mindful of now,
And really take it all in.
Your feet are standing in the present,
Not where you have, or have not been.
Take a deep breath and start to enjoy
What's right in front of your nose.
The people, the experiences, the great expectations,
That are out there to help you grow."
–*Be Where Your Feet Are*, by Julia Cook

Life gets so busy that sometimes we end up missing out on the world around us. We've all heard the saying "Take time to smell the flowers." Our world is a beautiful place and every day it gives us gifts to enjoy, but the only way to unwrap those gifts is to spend the time needed to notice them.

I was given the gift of laughter a few years back when I visited a school in Alaska. I pulled my car into the parking lot one morning and there right in front of me was a great big HUGE moose.

Apparently, I made a very dangerous decision (note: we don't have moose in Nebraska) when I got out of my car and walked right up to him. "You are absolutely gorgeous," I said to him, as he snorted, turned, and walked away.

As I was walking in through the front door of the school, I ran into a very anxious-looking principal with a bull horn in one hand and her cell phone in another.

"Are you Julia Cook?" she asked.

"Yep," I said.

"Please go wait for me in my office! I can't talk to you right now. We have a moo . . ." she said as she walked past me abruptly.

"Yeah, I thought to myself . . . I met him in the parking lot. He's beautiful!"

Shortly after, I watched out the window as the chaos began. The police department, fire department, and the department of natural resources started showing up, all equipped with stun guns. They carefully stood in formation making an adult-lined pathway. When the school bus arrived, the kids were quickly ushered through the pathway into the school. A few minutes later, the principal came into her office.

"That damn moose!" she said. "Do you know what he did?"

"No," I hesitantly replied.

"He had the audacity to make my playground his mating area!!! MY PLAY-GROUND!" she said.

"How do you know?" I asked.

"Oh, let me tell you how! When a moose wants to mark his 'mating area,' he digs a hole, pees in the hole, and makes pee mud, and then rolls in it! Then he calls in the cows, and surprisingly, they show up!"

She grabbed a pen and a napkin and began drawing a diagram.

"He made a hole here, here, and here. My school is here! Right in the middle!"

"Do you even know what that means, Julia Cook?"

I apprehensively shook my head. All I could think about was PEE MUD, and how glad I am my husband doesn't do that for me!

"It means NO OUTDOOR RECESS FOR A FULL WEEK! (Apparently, this is a really big deal in Alaska!)"

During lunch, I overheard one of the teachers say, "If you get in their way during mating season, they'll kill you."

Note to self: The next time you see a moose in a parking lot, find another parking lot.

What a mindful experience of an unusual day. One that still makes me laugh out loud every time I see a mud puddle.

Becoming more aware of the beautiful world we are living in can help you start to appreciate what really matters to you. It can also enhance your attention skills, lessen job burnout, make sleeping easier, and improve your overall health.[6]

Take a little time out every day to "Be Where Your Feet Are."

- Use all of your senses – sight, smell, sound, touch, and taste to experience parts of your day. Remark on the unusual. Enjoy the changing seasons. Be curious.
- Be on the lookout for joy in simple pleasures.
- Be as good to yourself as you are to your close friends.
- When you have negative thoughts, take a minute to close your eyes, take in a few deep breaths, and clear your head.

Get Your Move On

Physical activity helps promote feelings of well-being because it triggers the release of endorphins (feel-good chemicals) in the brain. To me, being "physically active" sounds painful. So instead, I like to say joyfully active.

If you can find physically engaging, enjoyable things to do, staying active feels like an invitation – as opposed to an obligation. Some of my favorites include working in my yard, Pilates, going on walks with friends, riding E-bikes (makes me feel like I have the rubber legs of a seven-year-old), dancing (when nobody is

[6]Mayo Clinic Staff, "Mindfulness Exercises," Mayo Clinic, October 11, 2022, https://www.mayoclinic.org/healthy-lifestyle/consumer-health/in-depth/mindfulness-exercises/art-20046356.

watching), playing sports of any kind, and cleaning my house with my earbuds in (Jimmy Buffett can make any situation fun – even toilet brushing!).

Also, don't forget to flood your brain with oxygen by taking in really deep breaths periodically throughout the day and S-T-R-E-T-C-H every time you get a chance so all of your muscles remember what they're supposed to do.

Speaking of stretching . . . In the late '80s and early '90s, my middle school principal went to a "Benefits of Periodic Stretching" conference for kids. It made a huge impact on him (like every other conference he attended), so he convinced all of us that our whole school needed to take time out every day to S-T-R-E-T-C-H.

His idea was to have random music play over the speaker system for about 15 to 20 seconds 4 to 5 times throughout the school day. When we heard the music, everyone was asked to stop what they were doing, stand up, take in a few deep breaths, and stretch until the music stopped.

This plan was going over quite well, and both teachers and kids were loving it. But on Monday of week three, I happened to be standing in the copy room near the office when I heard Color Me Badd's song "I Wanna Sex You Up" blast over the speaker system.

I ran into my principal's office and said, "What are you doing??? Turn it off! Turn it off!"

My principal smiled as he reached down to touch his toes. "Why?" he said. "I just love this song . . . I wanna set you up . . ."

"No, no, turn it off!"

"I wanna set you up!"

"It doesn't say *set* . . . It says I wanna SEX you up!"

The happy on his face turned to sheer horror and brutal embarrassment as he quickly reached for the off button of his boom box.

Then he looked at me with terror in his eyes and said, "Shit!"

All I could do was bust out laughing, and after he started to breathe again, he tried hard not to let me see him laugh – but he couldn't hold it in either.

Of course, every kid in the school went home and told their parents about the event, but this was the '80s, a time long before the existence of social media, and the parents didn't believe a word the kids said.

Every day you need to find ways to stay joyfully active.

Stretch! Move! Laugh!

And don't forget to stay hydrated. The human brain is made up of 75% water. Becoming even slightly dehydrated can cause you to develop a headache, become irritable, and lower your cognitive function.

It seems like every time we feel a headache coming on, we reach for our favorite over-the counter-remedy. Save your liver and your kidneys. The minute your head starts to hurt, drink an entire bottle of water before you self-medicate, and wait 10–15 minutes to see if your pain goes away.

Sometimes the simplest solution to a physical ailment is also the most effective.

Keep Learning

Researchers are always searching for a cure for dementia. A recent review of published research found "encouraging but inconclusive" evidence that three types of behavioral interventions can help prevent dementia: controlling your blood pressure, physical activity, and continued cognitive training.[7]

The brain is like a muscle: "use it or lose it!"

Learning every day will keep your brain in great shape, make your more confident, and boost your self-worth.

Here's a few things you can do to keep learning. (More are listed at the end of the chapter.)

- Research a topic or learn a new skill of interest to you.
- Work on a jigsaw puzzle. Jigsaw puzzles build inductive, deductive, and spatial orientation reasoning skills.
- Try two recipes. (Then if you botch one you can still say, "Look what I made!")

When I was six, I started taking accordion lessons. When I turned seven, I got a unicycle for my birthday. I put these two skills together at the age of 10. When I turned 55, I wanted to see if I could still master my unique skill set. You can actually watch a video of the results of this endeavor on YouTube.

Why did I include this you ask? Well, if you ever question your own mental wellness, remember there's a woman out there playing the accordion on a unicycle.

Give

A few months ago, I was pulling into a Starbucks drive-thru in my hometown when a police car turned left right in front of me, almost clipping my bumper. The officer drove up to the speaker and ordered. I followed and quickly wrote down his patrol car number.

I was *so* mad. I was going to call and report this rude, reckless guy. How dare he! He's supposed to serve the public not cut them off in traffic!

---

[7]National Academics of Sciences, Engineering and Medicine, Consensus Study Report – Preventing Cognitive Decline and Dementia, "Evidence Supporting Three Interventions That Might Slow Cognitive Decline and the Onset of Dementia Is Encouraging but Insufficient to Justify a Public Health Campaign Focused on Their Adoption," News Release, June 22, 2017. https://www.nationalacademies.org/news/2017/06/evidence-support ing-three-interventions-that-might-slow-cognitive-decline-and-the-onset-of-dementia-is-encouraging-but-insufficient-to-justify-a-public-health-campaign-focused-on-their-adoption.

By the time I placed my order and turned the corner to drive up to the window, the cop car was quickly exiting the parking lot. I held out my Starbucks card to pay, and the person at the window said, "Oh, your coffee is free today. Officer Scotty bought your drink. He does it for someone every morning, and today's your lucky day!"

Wow, was I shocked. I felt so bad for misjudging the guy. It really bothers me when I get so negative sometimes.

A few days later, I was still feeling bad, so I drove to a different Starbucks thinking I would pay it forward and be more like Officer Scotty.

"I'll pay for the car behind me," I said.

"Ok, that will be $85.49."

What????

The guy bought for his whole office. I ended up paying a lot forward. (Note to self: Always ask before you offer, and if it's too much, try doing it on another day.)

The point being, doing nice things for others without expecting anything back is a great way to feel better about yourself. Giving in any form creates an inner significance, which makes us feel more satisfied with life because it reminds us that we matter. There are so many ways to give. You can volunteer to help with a service project, share a kind thought, or simply smile to let another person know they are important enough to get noticed.

We all need to feel significant, and making a positive difference in the life of someone else can be a mental wellness game changer!

Worth Remembering

- Building mental wellness is a process that takes time. Remember the importance of small steps along the way.
- Everyone has a unique recipe for building their mental wellness, and every recipe requires five main ingredients:

  1. CONNECT
  2. TAKE NOTICE
  3. MOVE
  4. KEEP LEARNING
  5. GIVE

Worth Trying

- Make a conscious effort to talk to and with **people**.
- Schedule a catch-up call with friends who **add to your life**.
- Seek out joy and hidden pleasures.
- Do something nice for someone without expecting anything in return.
- Smile with kind eyes. (Note: if you have resting bitch face, you know who you are, and it isn't your fault! Practice smiling big in the mirror so that what others end up seeing is truly how you feel.)
- Volunteer in an area <u>NOT</u> directly related to school. We volunteer already at school . . . sometimes A LOT!
- Donate to a charity or help out with a project you **believe in**.
- Learn to play an instrument. (It's never too late to learn.)
- Fix up an old bike or an old car.
- Redo a room in your house via DIY.
- Take time to S-T-R-E-T-C-H throughout the day. (These are the stretches my principal used.)
  - NECK AND SHOULDER STRETCH – Stand straight, feet together. Lock fingers, palms down, and reach up above your head as high as you can above your head. As you reach up, tuck your chin down to elongate your spine.
  - HIP FLEXOR STRENGTHENER – Place one hand against a wall to steady yourself as you mimic sitting down. Cross one leg over the other forming two right angles, one leg resting on the other. with one leg crossed over the other. Sit and hold for 10 seconds, then switch.

- **CORE STRETCHER** – Stand up tall with your arms out wide. Lean back while looking straight up and arch your back toward the ground.
- **OBLIQUE STRENGTHENER** – Kneel down on one knee. Reach the opposite arm above your head and slowly arch your body to that side. Then switch to the other side.

03 Building a Teacher's Bag of Tricks

"Teaching is a form of art, based on science. It's brain science with an artistic delivery."

–Julia Cook

On day one of my student teaching experience, my cooperating teacher showed me a visual I will never forget. Sitting on a table was a 55-gallon garbage bag overstuffed and overflowing with wadded-up paper, barely tied shut with a string. Next to the big bag was a clear, snack-sized mini zip bag with 5–10 tiny pieces of torn paper inside.

"This is my bag of teaching tricks," he said as he lifted the big bag off of the table with pride. "It has taken me over 28 years to fill this up."

He handed me the snack bag.

"This is your teaching bag of tricks because you're just starting out. The best teachers are eternal learners who are always on the lookout for good tricks to put in their bag. You'll never know it all, and that's the magic, because you can always get better at what you do! If your bag ever stops growing, it's time to quit teaching and do something else. My goal is that when you are done with student teaching, this little bag will be so full, you'll need a sandwich bag."

Looking back, I realize he was right. We can't ever stop finding great teaching tricks. If we do, we'll turn into one of those stick-in-the-mud teachers we've all had, and wished we didn't.

Top 10 Tricks

Here are 10 of the best tricks I have in my bag. Feel free to give them a try, and if they really work for you, please share them with others.

#1 Relationships! Relationships! Relationships!

Kids before content, *always*.

One day, a six-year-old boy came into my office with huge emotions, and a very heavy heart.

"My parents are getting divorced and it's all my fault!"

"Oh, no. There is no way this is your fault," I immediately said. "There are only two reasons why people get divorced: either they can't trust each other anymore or they can't find a way to talk to each other. Here, I'll make you a list."

I pulled out a sheet of paper, wrote this down, and handed it to him.

"Look . . . is your name on the list?" The boy studied the list for a few moments.

"Nope," he said.

"Then there is no way this divorce can be your fault!"

The boy took in a deep breath of relief, nodded yes, and then looked me right in the eye and said, "Yeah, Mrs. Cook, you're probably right. . . . It's definitely a *trust* issue."

"Why do you say that?" I asked.

"Cuz my mama's a ho!"

SHOCK!

Never did I expect those words to come out of his mouth!

But, once that young boy realized he was in no way responsible for the divorce, he was able to wrap his head around the situation. From then on, we talked about relationships and how they work . . . or in this case, why they stop working.

Every human relationship must have two things to thrive: **trust** and **communication**. If a relationship you are involved in isn't working, ask yourself "Is this a trust issue, a communication problem, or both?" Once you identify where the gaps are, you can channel your resources in the direction needed to strengthen the relationship.

Teaching is a profession revolving around relationships. To do your job effectively, you must be able to talk to your kids in a way they can understand you and trust them to follow your lead. In return, your students must be able to effectively communicate their needs and trust you will do everything in your power to meet those needs.

Your effectiveness as a teacher depends most heavily on the relationships you build with the kids in your class. Without your students, you wouldn't have a job!

Your students should always be more important to you than the material you are presenting to them.

You are teaching kids content.

You are not teaching content to kids.

In addition, you must also be able to develop functional relationships with parents, your colleagues, and your administration.

Mark Sanborn, author of *The Fred Factor*, shares the 7 B's needed to successfully build and strengthen your relationships with others.[1]

Be Real – Don't try to impress others. Just practice being your unique self. Authenticity is crucial to building trust.

Be Genuinely Interested in Others – Focus conversations on how best you meet the needs of the person you are talking to. Interested people always attract appreciation.

Be a Better Listener – Make the person you are talking to feel seen and heard by actively listening to what they are saying. When you listen whole-heartedly to what someone else is saying you can learn a lot more about them.

Be Empathetic – Feeling understood and validated is one of our highest human needs. Being empathetic is having the ability to see the world through another person's eyes.

Be Honest – Dishonesty destroys trust, which is a crucial component to every relationship. In situations where being honest is painfully difficult, use kind words and only say what needs to be said. Never make promises you are unable to keep.

Be Helpful – Do nice things to help others without expecting anything in return.

Be Prompt – When you are late, you are telling others your time is more valuable than theirs. Do everything in your power to always be 10 minutes early. Then if something suddenly comes up, you have some wiggle room.

---

[1]Sanborn, Mark, *The Fred Factor: How Passion in Your Work and Life Can Turn the Ordinary into the Extraordinary*, Crown Currency, 2004.

#2 Be Ready When the Kids Walk Through the Door

"Life" happens, and unexpected events in our personal lives can change our daily plans in a hot minute. Sometimes, just making it to school is a heroic accomplishment. That said, if you do your prep work the night before, when your students enter your classroom in the morning and throughout the day, your focus can be on them, as opposed the content you plan to teach.

So many times, I see teachers in the copy room scrambling at the last minute, trying to get the day's activities ready. They race down the hallway and enter their rooms with an armful of freshly copied papers just as their kids are walking in.

Unfortunately, they end up missing out on one of the most important parts of the day . . . greeting their kids.

"Hi! How are you today!"

"Nice shoes!"

"I'm so glad you feel better. We missed you!"

"How's your mom?"

"How did your soccer game go last night?"

"I'm so happy to see you!"

"Wow, thanks for walking in so quietly."

"You look like you need a hug. Rough morning?"

"Thanks for coming today. I love it when you're here."

Being there 100% when your kids walk through the door demonstrates your authentic presence. It tells your students they are far more important than what you are planning to teach them. Your full attention allows them to be your priority. It also gives you a great read on the struggles and celebrations they are carrying into your classroom, making climate control proactive.

On chaotic days when life trumps the best of your intentions and forces you to prep on the fly, take just five minutes before you start teaching and do a quick version of your usual meet and greet.

"How's your day going so far? Does anyone have anything they'd like to share? Any highs? (Highs are the best things that have happened lately.) *Any lows?* (Lows are the worst things that have happened lately.) *Any sprinkles?* (Sprinkles are ways that you have either given or received kindness.)"

By doing this, your students will realize they really do matter and you genuinely care about them.

This all sounds great on paper, but everyone who is reading this knows the true reality: We often can't find enough hours in the day to get everything done! Unfortunately, we can't add more hours to our day, but we can get more strategic with how we choose to spend our time. Here are a few time-saving tips that might be helpful:

- Make a classroom and task "TO DO" list each day and check it off as you go
- Create an ongoing supply list for items you are going to need at school.
- Delegate classroom chores (watering plants, straightening toys or books, organizing supplies, etc.) to your students.
- Keep an extra mini-stash of supplies in your room so you don't have to run to the office when you run out of things.
- Do one thing at a time – multitasking slows down your performance and actually ends up wasting your time.
- Create an organized "Save It" file for every effective lesson you prepare so you can tweak it and use it the following year.
- Collaborate – Ask other good teachers to share their lesson ideas with you and be willing to share yours with them if asked. Remember, teaching kids is not a competition, it's a collaboration!"
- Have everything ready for the next day before you leave school.

#3 Creatively Reposition the Talkers

Kids LOVE to talk to each other . . . especially when they are supposed to be listening. It seems like they do it now more than ever! I used to think, "How rude! Hey, you, please be quiet! It's my turn to talk. Why aren't you listening? Where are your manners?"

But after doing almost four thousand school visits, I now understand rudeness is rarely my young audience's intent.

Always keep in mind . . . *Every student misbehavior you encounter results from an unmet need.*

Kids often talk when I'm speaking because they believe what they are saying to each other is much more important than what I am saying to them. Sometimes, they talk to seek attention. Some kids are still developing their conversational skills and have not yet internalized the concept of "it is not my turn to talk."

Also, something they hear me say may trigger an experience and they can't resist telling their neighbor all about it – right during the best part of my presentation! Whatever the reason, it is challenging! But as Lori L. Desautels says in her essential book, *Connections Over Compliance*, "Behavior management is not about students. Behavior management is about the adults."[2]

To combat this phenomenon, I came up with an idea that really works. . . . I move them. Right in the middle of a sentence, if I see a kid talking or not tracking

[2]Desautels, Lori L., *Connections Over Compliance*, Wyatt-MacKenzie Publishing, Deadwood, Oregon, 2020, p. 33.

for a period of time, I invite them to a new space: "Hey, I need you to sit right here because I might need you later." Or suggest, "Hey, that spot's not working for you. This is a much better view!"

I go over to the kid and gently take their hand and relocate them to a different area – often where they don't know the kids around them. Then, I immediately continue talking while they are walking to their new spot and getting situated. Kids do not feel embarrassed or singled out. They are not looked down upon; they are simply just relocated.

I flash them periodic, authentic smiles throughout the rest of the presentation, which validates that they are not being shamed or punished. Instead, they begin to feel important and more included.

The relocation comes off as an *opportunity* as opposed to a *punishment*. Kids don't see it coming, and moving them away from the person they are comfortable talking to works miracles. Then, if I get a chance to use them for a shining moment later on, I make sure to tell them what great listeners they have been.

I once made a huge mistake by saying at the beginning of my talk, "I really need you to listen. If you are talking I might move you to a better spot so you can get more out of today." Ninety-eight percent of the kids started talking . . . just to see what I would do. It was a disaster! (Note to self: Don't announce it—just do it. Even mid-sentence.)

After a few relocations, kids start to police themselves. I once heard a kid say, "Be quiet or she'll move me!"

#4 Build Your Lessons Around Your Most Challenging Students

If your most active kid only has a five-minute attention span and needs to be on the move, consider gearing your whole class instruction time to five minutes or less.

If your delivery time and/or mode is geared toward your middle or high-ability learners, you will naturally lose engagement from some of your students and invite them into the land of off-task behavior.

In his book *Lost at School*, Ross W. Greene makes the case that challenging behavior can be a detriment to kids by way of how other classmates view that student.[3] So, what if you build your lessons around your most challenging students? As Greene says, "What if challenging kids were not solely in the position of needing help, but were also in the position to provide it?"

---

[3]Greene, Ross W., *Lost at School*, Scribner, New York, 2014, pp. 180–181.

Also, physically model and demonstrate what you would like your students to do as you explain it to them. This is much more impactful than verbal instructions alone; e.g., *"When you are finished with your math papers, please walk them over to this basket and put them in here like this."*

Everyone learns more effectively when they experience new knowledge through multiple modes, even if one mode is preferred.

#5 Call on Every Kid

Create a system where every child gets randomly called on.

We often call on those who have their hands raised, and the quieter kids and underachievers become complacent with not needing to respond, and/or become less willing to self-advocate. To avoid making some kids feel uncomfortable, try this trick in conjunction with the *phone-a-friend* concept.

Write each students' name on a wide craft stick with permanent marker and have the kids decorate their sticks. Then place the sticks in a jar and draw from the jar when you are wanting to have kids participate or answer a question.

After answering, place the stick in a second jar so you can cycle thru asking every child. Always allow kids the option to use the *phone-a-friend*. If a child is anxious or reluctant to participate: they can use their voice to ask another student to work with them, or take over their turn instead.

#6 Teaching with a "Get-To" Mentality

We all like to be told what we GET TO do, but very few of us like to be told what we HAVE TO do. GET-TOs are opportunities, and HAVE-TOs are orders. We naturally gear more effective thinking toward positivity and opportunity, so it's all in how you say it:

"We get to do our math now so we can get it done before we go outside for recess." vs "You have to do your math or you can't go out!"

"I'm so excited to tell you what we get to do today," vs "We have a lot of work to do today!"

Or, how about this one:

"You know the word TEST stands for *Think Every Situation Through*. I am so excited for you! You get to take this test, and you get to show the entire state of "(your state here)" how amazing you are! TEST also stands for *Terrific Every Single Time*! and I know you all have what it takes to be TERRIFIC! Now let's do this!" vs "Today we have a very important test to take and you have to do your very best on it!"

Teaching itself is a GET-TO, not a HAVE-TO profession!

It's a golden opportunity because you GET TO work with our future! If you develop a "Have to go to work" mentality, the magical gifts of teaching turn into the humdrum obligations of a job.

#7 Proximity: It's *with* Not *At.*

I've found when I speak, both to kids and to adults, talking *with* my audience is much more impactful than talking *at* them.

Close proximity is a magnet for attention.

When I'm doing a keynote, I walk around the attendees as I talk, as opposed to speaking from a podium. This allows my audience to see, hear, and feel my authenticity even more effectively.

When I read a story to kids that's projected onto a screen, I sit right next to them on the floor. This models authenticity, and shows my audience I'm willing to look through their lens.

If I do a demo of a concrete visual, I kneel down closer to the floor, and the kids naturally start to lean in to watch.

If I have something important to say to a child individually, I have found they will listen much more intently if I position my eyes lower than theirs and talk up to them. This helps to build a willing confidence and state of comfort in the listener.

Overpowering kids with a physical, assumingly overbearing stance, often puts them on the defensive. Also, eye-level contact at times may come off as seeming competitive.

Try talking up to your students! It's a great way to proactively get into their heads!

#8 Never Yell–Unless It's an Emergency

A great teacher never has to raise their voice.

Yeah, right. I can see you rolling your eyes. Kids get loud. Then we get louder trying to talk over them. Since they outnumber us, we end up losing our voice – and our effectiveness.

I once was told, "Yelling is like swearing . . . the more you do it, the less effective it is." And it's true.

There are times when raising your voice is necessary, especially when it comes to safety. When you truly need to yell, you need it to work!

Using *Chat Backs* is a great way to grab kids' attention.

A Chat Back is part of a short phrase or part of a song broken into two parts. The teacher says the first half and the kids then complete the phrase in unison. At the end of the Chat Back the focus is on you. Chat Backs can be as simple as "Class, Class" . . . "We are here!" or as fun as "We will, we will" . . . "ROCK YOU!" Some teachers gear their Chat Backs around the theme of their classroom. Others use lines from movies, riddles, or songs.

The trick to getting the kids to buy into a Chat Back is to brainstorm creative ideas with your class and have them decide as a group which ones to use. The more you involve your students in the creation of your Chat Backs, the more effective they will be. Also, make sure your Chat Back is short, catchy, and fun to say. Overused Chat Backs can easily become monotonous and ineffective, so change them up often.

If your students need even more motivation to use Chat Backs effectively, create a reward system like this: Fill a clear container with cotton balls and set it next to a clear container marked "WIN!" of the same size. Each time your class completes a successful Chat Back, ask one student to move a cotton ball from the full jar to the "WIN!" Jar. When the "WIN!" jar is full, celebrate a predetermined and agreed-upon class reward.

Examples of class rewards are an extra recess, choice of activity, free assignment pass, choice of seating for the day, popcorn party, outdoor math, etc.

Keep in mind, the more involved your students are with determining the reward, the harder they will work to earn it!

#9 Start Every Day with a Clean Slate

How would you like to be welcomed when you walk into a classroom? Put yourself in the shoes of your students:

"Today is a brand-new day! I can't wait to see what you are going to do with it. Yesterday must have been hard for you, so today we start over. Today, you get a clean slate! Remember, your job in my class is to add to what we are doing, not take from it and if you find yourself taking, you might have to leave again for a bit, but you can always come back. This is a safe place for you and I want you in here, so show me what I know you can do!!"

vs

"You're sitting here today. I've moved your desk away from everybody else so you won't be disruptive. Maybe now you can keep your hands and feet to yourself and not bug others like you did yesterday. Don't test me, or you're going straight to the principal's office."

Giving your students a clean slate when they walk through your classroom door is a great way to say, "I believe in you, and I know you can be successful today." Remember, hopeful teachers grow hopeful learners!"

How can we expect our kids to believe in themselves if they think we don't believe they can do it?

#10 Better the Ball!

Think about the game of volleyball.

The setter strategically places herself in front of the net and waits for a pass.

Sometimes the ball comes right to her . . . perfect pass. She doesn't have to move her feet at all! All she has to do is stand there and wait for the ball. Then, she sets it up to a hitter.

Most of the time, the ball is passed out of system and it doesn't come right to her, so she has to move her feet and position herself underneath the ball to set it.

Once in a while, the ball is a shanked pass and it's heading out of bounds fast.

The setter does everything she can to pop that ball up and keep it from hitting the floor.

Sometimes it works . . . and sometimes it doesn't.

Regardless of the outcome, the setter peels herself off of the floor and prepares herself for the next pass. She doesn't walk off the court hanging her head because there is more game to come and she knows she did her best.

Teaching is a lot like volleyball.

The kids are the ball, the parents are the passers, the peers are the hitters, and *you* are the setter.

You cannot control how the ball is passed to you. You cannot control what the hitter does with the ball after you set it up for success. All you can control is *you*.

Do you do everything in your power to *Better the Ball* when it's in your hands?

Is that child better off because of time spent with you than they would have been without you? If so, that's a win . . . and that's enough!

So many times, we own and act on worries we cannot control. This wastes our strengths and channels our energy ineffectively, making teaching overwhelming.

Be the teacher that BETTERS THE BALL!

You won't win every point.

You won't win every game.

But you will win the overall match!

Worth Remembering

- The best teachers are eternal learners who are always on the lookout for good tricks to put in their bag. You'll never know it all, and that's the magic, because you can always get better at what you do!
- Your students should always be more important than the material you are presenting to them. You are teaching kids content. You are not teaching content to kids.
- There are 7 B's to Relationship Building. They are: BE REAL, BE GENUINELY INTERESTED IN OTHERS, BE A BETTER LISTENER, BE EMPATHETIC, BE HONEST, BE HELPFUL, and BE PROMPT.
- Teach with a "GET-TO" mentality. "GET-TO's" are opportunities. "HAVE-TO's" are orders.
- Yelling is like swearing . . . the more you do it, the less effective it is.
- TEST stands for Think Every Situation Through so you can do Terrific Every Single Time.

Worth Trying

- Start each day with a clean slate.
- If kids are talking when you are giving direct instructions, quickly move them to a different location in the room and immediately continue teaching without skipping a beat.
- Build your lessons around your students who have the shortest attention span.

Hopeful Teachers Grow Hopeful Kids

> "A man begins to die when he ceases to expect anything from tomorrow."
>
> *–Abraham Miller*

Teaching today's kids can be challenging. Last week, a teacher friend of mine said, "I feel like I'm swimming upstream, in a river of thick molasses!" Educators everywhere report feeling anxious, fearful, worried, overwhelmed, and sad.[1] Yet somehow, we find a way to keep going.

What's the secret ingredient to owning a positive and productive attitude while enduring the current adverse scenarios that are plaguing our thoughts? HOPE!

Hope is an overall perception that one's goals can be met.[2] Hope is not only an emotion, it's an optional way of thinking. It ignites the idea that tomorrow is going to be better than today, and I have the power to make that happen.

Keeping Your Tank Full

I like to think of hope as being the fuel inside of a gas tank. You can have the most powerful race car in the world, but if you don't have gas in the tank, your car won't have the energy it needs to go anywhere.

---

[1]Eva, Amy L., "Three Ways to Feel More Hopeful as an Educator," *Greater Good Science Center Magazine*, September 13, 2022, https://greatergood.berkeley.edu/article/item/three_ways_to_feel_more_hopeful_as_an_educator.

[2]Slater, Carleigh B., "Snyder's hope theory: A beacon for teachers contending with secondary stress, compassion fatigue and burnout in relation to students' experiences of abuse," *Child Protection and Practice* 1, no. 1, April 2024, https://www.sciencedirect.com/science/article/pii/S295019382400007X.

Hope is a powerful force that can transform both our lives and the lives of our students.

It can be a never-ending resource. It gives us the energy we need to turn our goals into realities. When things get tough, we use our hope to get tougher.

When I first met Phillip (AKA Philly), he was an extremely smart and bubbly kindergartener with bright, steel green eyes. Philly was diagnosed with muscular dystrophy at the age of three. By the time he started kindergarten he needed leg braces and crutches to walk . . . or should I say run. Nothing seemed to stop Philly from being like everybody else, and I mean nothing! The gleam in his eyes screamed "I CAN do that . . . just watch me!"

Four years later, I got a call from Philly's mom.

"We don't know what to do, Mrs. Cook. Philly is refusing to do his work at school. He won't participate in class. He won't have anything to do with his friends. He talks back to his teachers, and his attitude toward everything is awful. Can you please meet with him? We don't know what to do or say anymore. I know we are losing our boy, and he is losing his body, but I never thought I'd see the day when he lost his will to try."

I checked with Philly's teacher to see what was happening in the class. His teacher was one month into her first year, and was doing everything she could to basically survive.

"I'm at a loss!" she said. "I really don't know what to do with Philly. At the beginning of school, he was great. Now, he isn't trying at all especially in math – his best subject. He won't engage with other kids, he refuses to do his work, and if I push him, he gets really angry with me. I know he's smart. In fact, sometimes, I think he's smarter than I am. I can see it in his eyes. How do I teach him when he doesn't feel like learning has a purpose?"

The next morning, Philly rolled into my office. He was slumped down into his wheelchair. His hair was covering his eyes and was awkwardly trapped between his glasses and his face.

"What's up Philly?" I said.

"Nothing."

"I talked with your mom and your teacher yesterday. They are really worried about you. They both say you've quit trying."

"I have."

"Why?"

Philly brushed the hair away from his face with the back of his hand and looked up at me. His steel green eyes were unusually dull, and tears began rolling down his cheeks.

"Why should I try, Cook? Why should I do anything? What's the point? No matter what I do or how hard I work, it won't do any good. It's not like I'm going to grow up and be somebody. I probably won't even be here next year."

Philly spoke the raw truth. His words gutted me to the core. My toes filled with lead. The gas in Philly's tank was almost gone, and this horrible disease had super glued his gas cap shut. Philly was running on fumes, and there wasn't anything anyone could do or say to change that.

"Do you like your teacher, Philly?"

"Yes, she's really nice, and she tries hard to help me, but I wish she'd stop. I just want to be left alone."

"You've always been really good at math right?"

"Yes. It's super easy, especially this year."

"Well, I know there are a few kids in your class who really struggle at math. What if we talk to your teacher and ask her if you can get your assignment done fast and then help other kids with their work? Sometimes kids can explain stuff to other kids better than grownups can."

"Like a tutor?"

"Kind of like a tutor."

Philly's face lit up and his steel green eyes started to smile.

"Sure! I can do that!"

This was a true aha moment for Philly. He started to do his work in class again, and he really tried to do his best . . . not for himself, but to help out his peers. Philly started feeling significant again. Instead of thinking only about himself, he focused on making others feel more valued.

We continued to meet once a week to process our sneaky plan . . . and it worked! After a few weeks, Philly started helping out his mom more at home. His whole demeanor improved even more because he realized even with his diagnosis, he had the power to make others feel worthy.

Unfortunately, fourth grade ended up being Philly's last year of school.

I never found a way to thank Philly for the priceless gifts he gave me because Muscular Dystrophy took him all too soon. But he left a lasting legacy. He showed me firsthand how powerful hope is. More importantly, he challenged me to figure out a way for him to survive after his hope ran out.

The Power of Hope

Some of the most credible research on hope was conducted in the 1950s by Dr. Curt Richter of Johns Hopkins University. Richter demonstrated that hope is a lead contributor to building perseverance and resilience by conducting numerous experiments involving the drowning, or near drowning, of both domestic and wild rats.[3]

In one experiment, he placed both domestic and wild rats in vats of water. The rats would dive to the bottom to survey their situation, swim along the outside edge of the vat, and scratch at the sides attempting to climb out. Once the rats figured out there was not a way out of the vat, they would give up, stop swimming, and drown within two minutes.

Richter then assembled rising platforms inside of the vats of water. He would periodically raise the platforms up close enough to the surface so that the rats could touch the floor with their heads above water. This gave the rats hope that they could eventually escape. The rats in the raising platform vats swam nearly 24 hours before dying of exhaustion.

Humans and rats are not the same, but learning is learning.

Richter's research helps us understand the remarkable power of hope. When we have it, it can carry us through extreme circumstances. But, when we lose our hope, we give up, and we drown.

The challenges our kids are facing in today's world can be extremely difficult. Making the role of hope in education for both students and educators seem insurmountable. There are many facts about HOPE to keep in mind:

- Hope is a free resource. It's affordable to everyone.
- Hope is a choice. We get to choose whether we have it or not.

---

[3]Richter, Curt P., "On the Phenomenon of Sudden Death in Animals and Man," from the Psychobiological Laboratory, Johns Hopkins Medical School, Baltimore. Presented at the American Psychosomatic Society 1956 Annual Meeting, March 25, 1956, Boston, https://www.aipro.info/wp/wp-content/uploads/2017/08/phenomena_sudden_death.pdf.

- Hope is a difference maker that can be both learned and shared with others.
- Hope itself is not specific to gender, IQ, race, ethnicity, or income level. It is an equal opportunity resource available to everyone. However, risk factors such as lower income, higher unemployment, less education, more illness, and poorer nutrition may work to diminish hope and make it more difficult to attain.

How we think about the future is a key determinant of success in school, work, and life. Life's most important and desired behaviors and outcomes – showing up, increasing our productivity, boosting our well-being, enjoying good health, and living longer – are all dependent upon hope.

According to Gallup Poll research having hope leads to a boost in happiness, gains in academic performance, and an astounding bump in workplace outcomes.[4]

It's easy to confuse hope with both *wishful thinking* and *optimism*, but it's important to keep in mind that they are very different things.

Wishful thinking occurs when there is no connection personally to the future through ones' own efforts. Someone might think, "I wish I could win the lottery!" But if they don't take the time to buy a lottery ticket, the chances of winning are next to zero.

Optimism is an attitude (e.g., "Look on the bright side." "Every cloud has a silver lining."). It doesn't concern itself with real information about the future, and it doesn't have a specific goal. Optimism can foster good health and happiness, and buffer the intensity of stress and anxiety. But when unfortunate things happen, optimists can get stuck and become frustrated.

Hope is different. Hope contains the following core beliefs:

- The future will be better than the present.
- I have the power to make it happen.
- There are many different pathways I can take to get to my goal.
- Every pathway contains obstacles.

In his book *Making Hope Happen*, research psychologist Dr. Shane Lopez presents a unique way of analyzing hope. Dr. Lopez describes the concept of hope as a cycle.

---

[4]Lopez, Shane J., "Want More Productive Workers – Give Them Hope," CNBC, March 8, 2013, `https://www.cnbc.com/2013/03/08/want-more-productive-workers-give-them-hope.html`.

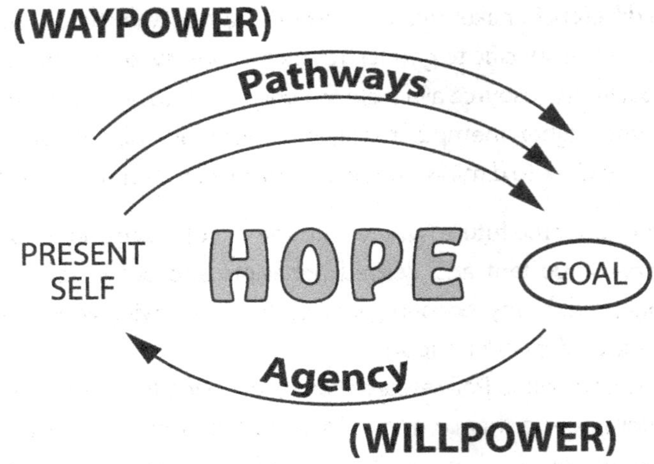

Hope happens when a combination of *willpower* and *waypower* work together in unison to propel your present self toward a goal.

Willpower is your inner voice that fuels your agency:

"I want to do it!"

"I will do it!"

"I can do it!"

"I did it!"

Willpower allows you to become the author of your own story.

Waypower is the plan you create to get to your goal.

Plans often contain many different pathways, but none of them are free of obstacles.

In his book, Lopez states that by the time a child is 10, the size of their hope cycle unit is set. When a child has experienced the benefits of hope in abundance prior to the age of 10, it results in a larger cycle unit, making goal achieving more probable. However, when hope has been scarcely experienced, the hope cycle unit is smaller, so achieving a goal becomes more difficult.

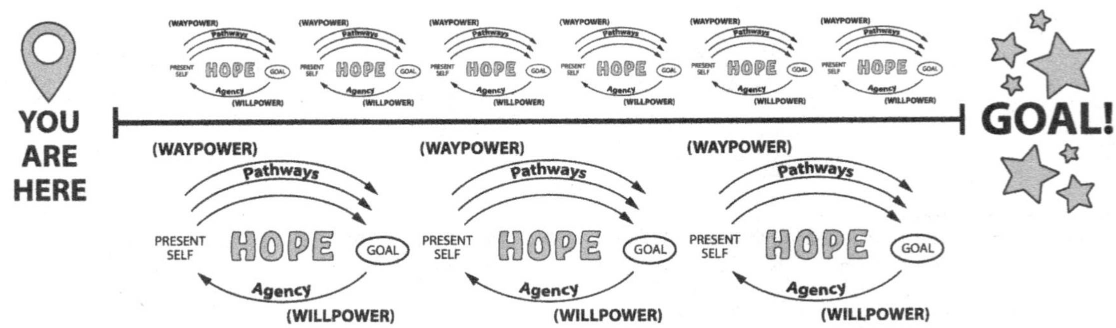

Lopez also explains the concept of *nexting*, which means talking about what you are going to do next. Nexting combined with our goals, agency, and pathways (willpower and waypower) gives us the tools and compulsion we need to simply finish what we start.

Shane Lopez understood the power of hope and the struggle of hopelessness on a highly intuitive level, and his unique idea leads us to ask two very important questions:

1. How can we build hope in kids and make their hope cycles bigger in size before the age of 10?
2. How can we improve the output of a hope cycle after the age of 10?

Building Hope

Hope is built by setting and achieving goals that MATTER to US.

You build hope every time you:

- Set a goal that really matters.
- Think of multiple ways to attain your goal.
- Carry out our plans to a satisfactory conclusion.
- Celebrate your achievement.

Hope in Action

While on a random flight to Houston, I was lucky enough to sit next to Monica Dixon, an amazing educator and professional trainer. She shared with me one of her many powerful stories about hope:

"I was the Dean of Students at one of the most diverse high schools in the state of Nebraska. It was late winter when James, one of my seniors, walked into my office and hesitantly sat down. Outside in the hallway, students moved through their day as usual. I distinctly remember hearing the soft hum of school settling into the season after he closed my door. James had finally hit a wall. He could no longer outrun the four-year truth he'd been carrying around. He was behind. Not by a little. There were twenty-one credits standing between James and graduation.

Until that day, James had shrugged off the issue, but as he sat across the desk from me, the full weight of reality landed in his lap. His body looked crumpled with defeat. His eyes were filled with tears, and his voice cracked as he told me what others had already decided. "They said I'm not going to make it, Ms. Dixon. They told me there is no way I can graduate and walk with my class. I'm too far behind, and I'll never be able to catch up. The option they gave me is to do summer school and hope it's enough or be a 2nd year senior. I don't want to do either of those!

I didn't rush him. Instead, I allowed him to be seen. Then, when the moment was right, I said, 'Well, if you really want this James, then let's create a plan. We'll take it one class at a time, and I will support you. There are no shortcuts to doing this. But what I can offer you is my hope. I believe in you. It's going to take your everything to get this done by May, but I honestly think you have what it takes to make it happen.

James began the next day. He arrived early. He stayed late. He used his lunch breaks and weekends. One class at a time, he chipped away at the distance. I checked in often. Not to push. Not to rescue. But to remind him that I was there. There were many difficult days. Days when the goal felt like an eternity away. But hope is not loud, it lives in quiet persistence. When it is held with structure and care, hope has the power to move mountains."

By spring, something shifted. What once felt impossible evolved into something real. By the time May arrived, James stood ready for a graduation walk he had genuinely earned.

About a month later, I received an email from James's English teacher:

"James is doing much better. The effort he has put forth since semester is insurmountable. As a senior assignment, I asked my students to write a personal narrative. I thought you might like to see his. You have obviously made a huge impact on his life.

Personal Narrative by James
The person I am today is not something that happened overnight. Matter of fact, it took me a lot of time, patience, and effort to get where I am today. It may sound crazy, but high school shaped the person I am.

As a freshman, nothing really seems important to you. You are fresh out of middle, still living in the mind of a child, but sooner or later comes a time when you have to grow up and take care of business. Some people catch on quicker than others though all it takes is a wake-up call. I was one of those kids, did none of the work and expected that everything would be handed to me like Halloween candy on October 31st. Sadly, it doesn't work that way.

My wake-up call happened in the middle of my senior year. Graduation was right around the corner; everyone was getting their caps and gown sizes, taking senior pictures, and there I was, trying to play catch up with others that chose to take the wrong route.

Like you can imagine, I was very frustrated about this. Time was running out and that due date was getting closer and closer. I had no idea what to do next. I went to see my school administrator, Mrs. Dixon, hoping she would give me some words of wisdom, and she did just that.

I explained to her how I had a million things on my plate and I if I couldn't get help to move forward, I was looking at summer school or even worse, becoming a 2nd year senior.

Mrs. Dixon explained to me that I can't allow myself to be stressed like this. She said thinking that I can get all the work done in a moment's notice is not a good plan. Then she helped me come up with a great plan to knock out each credit one by one. She told me she believed in me. This gave me the motivation I needed to stop feeling so down about myself and start thinking realistically. This new way of thinking from that day on put me in a position to graduate. What more could I ask for?"

Monica Dixon concluded her story by saying, "This is what hope can look like when someone believes in you enough to help you carry it. James added my hope to his own, and it gave him what he needed to power through."

Modeling Hope

Hope can be learned through modeling by significant people around you as well as through the natural consequences of your actions. To be an effective hope builder for others you must:

Be available – You have to be around to make a difference.

Be reliable – Don't promise what you can't deliver.

Anticipate the needs of others – Everyone has unique needs at different times.

Be an authentic presence – Kids know if you are faking it.

Offer physical contact when needed – Positive, healthy, boundary-respecting human touch is a must! (side hug, eye hug, elbow bump, fist bump, etc.).

Demonstrate courage – Trust yourself to try.

Be persistent – Don't go away . . . stay with it. Kids are worth it!

Have a growth mindset – Don't think of the glass as half full or half empty. . . . The glass is refillable!

Improving Hope Cycle Output

In order to make existing hope cycles more efficient, we first need to figure out a way to measure hope.

In fact, C. R. Snyder developed the Children's Hope Scale,[5] which asks kids a series of questions about how they see themselves.

HOW I SEE MYSELF...

(Children's Hope Scale)

1. I think I am doing pretty well.

None of the time	A little of the time	Some of the time	A lot of the time	Most of the time	All of the time
○	○	○	○	○	○

2. I can think of many ways to get the things in life that are most important to me.

None of the time	A little of the time	Some of the time	A lot of the time	Most of the time	All of the time
○	○	○	○	○	○

3. I am doing just as well as other kids my age.

None of the time	A little of the time	Some of the time	A lot of the time	Most of the time	All of the time
○	○	○	○	○	○

4. When I have a problem, I can come up with lots of ways to solve it.

None of the time	A little of the time	Some of the time	A lot of the time	Most of the time	All of the time
○	○	○	○	○	○

5. I think the things I have done in the past will help me in the future.

None of the time	A little of the time	Some of the time	A lot of the time	Most of the time	All of the time
○	○	○	○	○	○

6. Even when others want to quit, I know that I can find ways to solve the problem.

None of the time	A little of the time	Some of the time	A lot of the time	Most of the time	All of the time
○	○	○	○	○	○

To measure a child's WILLPOWER, you look at how they answer questions 1, 3, and 5.

---

[5] Snyder, C.R. et al., "The development and validation of the Children's Hope Scale," *Journal of Pediatric Psychology* 22, no. 3 (June 1997): 399–421. doi: https://doi.org/10.1093/jpepsy/22.3.399. PMID: 9212556.

HOW I SEE MYSELF...

(Children's Hope Scale)

WILLPOWER

1. I think I am doing pretty well.

   ○ None of the time   ○ A little of the time   ○ Some of the time   ○ A lot of the time   ○ Most of the time   ○ All of the time

2. I can think of many ways to get the things in life that are most important to me.

   ○ None of the time   ○ A little of the time   ○ Some of the time   ○ A lot of the time   ○ Most of the time   ○ All of the time

3. I am doing just as well as other kids my age.

   ○ None of the time   ○ A little of the time   ○ Some of the time   ○ A lot of the time   ○ Most of the time   ○ All of the time

4. When I have a problem, I can come up with lots of ways to solve it.

   ○ None of the time   ○ A little of the time   ○ Some of the time   ○ A lot of the time   ○ Most of the time   ○ All of the time

5. I think the things I have done in the past will help me in the future.

   ○ None of the time   ○ A little of the time   ○ Some of the time   ○ A lot of the time   ○ Most of the time   ○ All of the time

6. Even when others want to quit, I know that I can find ways to solve the problem.

   ○ None of the time   ○ A little of the time   ○ Some of the time   ○ A lot of the time   ○ Most of the time   ○ All of the time

To measure WAYPOWER, analyze the answers from questions 2, 4, and 6.

This scale allows you to see what kids need to improve the output of their hope cycle. Do they need more motivational strategies? Do they need more pathway ideas/options? Or are they lacking in both? It's important to keep in mind that hope is reciprocal.

- Hopeful parents have hopeful children.
- Hopeful teachers grow hopeful students.
- Hopeful employers cultivate hopeful employees.

Unfortunately, in contrast:

- Hopeless parents have hopeless children.
- Hopeless teachers grow hopeless students.
- Hopeless employers cultivate hopeless employees.

HOW I SEE MYSELF...

(Children's Hope Scale)

WAYPOWER

1. I think I am doing pretty well.

○	○	○	○	○	○
None of the time	A little of the time	Some of the time	A lot of the time	Most of the time	All of the time

2. I can think of many ways to get the things in life that are most important to me.

○	○	○	○	○	○
None of the time	A little of the time	Some of the time	A lot of the time	Most of the time	All of the time

3. I am doing just as well as other kids my age.

○	○	○	○	○	○
None of the time	A little of the time	Some of the time	A lot of the time	Most of the time	All of the time

4. When I have a problem, I can come up with lots of ways to solve it.

○	○	○	○	○	○
None of the time	A little of the time	Some of the time	A lot of the time	Most of the time	All of the time

5. I think the things I have done in the past will help me in the future.

○	○	○	○	○	○
None of the time	A little of the time	Some of the time	A lot of the time	Most of the time	All of the time

6. Even when others want to quit, I know that I can find ways to solve the problem.

○	○	○	○	○	○
None of the time	A little of the time	Some of the time	A lot of the time	Most of the time	All of the time

Always keep in mind, hope is not left to chance. What makes the difference in whether someone's hope is turned on or left inert depends on your mindset. A fixed mindset ("I can't do it!") neutralizes hope. Negative messages deplete your agency and keep you stuck.

A growth mindset ("I can't do it yet . . .") is a natural companion to hope.

There are many things teachers can do to help children maximize their hope cycle outputs. First, find a way to link a child's current thinking, efforts, and learning to their future, and create excitement for what's ahead.

Second, we need to teach children specific multiple pathways to meaningful goals (AKA There's more than one way to milk a duck!).

Next, we must encourage children to develop a growth mindset that can knock down existing obstacles and blaze new pathways toward their goals.

You also need to teach kids how to reestablish goals when circumstances demand it. NEVER RUN OUT OF GOALS!

Always be on the recruiting lookout for hope builders. If you know what to look for, you can find them everywhere.

Encourage kids to become hope builders for each other. Helping others builds a powerful sense of confidence and significance within that enhances both willpower and waypower.

Finally, always remember, hope only grows if kids are actively connected with their future. We need our students to always be looking ahead, figuring out what needs to be improved, and working toward developing and acquiring skills and confidence to make those improvements happen.

Worth Remembering

- Hope is an overall perception that one's goals can be met.
- How we think about the future is a key determinant of success in school, work, and life.
- There is a difference between wishful thinking, optimism, and hope.
- By the time children are 10, the size of their HOPE CYCLE UNIT is set.
- Hope is RECIPRICOL.
- Hope is learned through molding provided by significant people around us as well as through natural consequences of our actions.

Worth Trying

- Incorporate growth mindset and the amazing POWER OF YET into every lesson. Don't be a "BRICK BRAIN" with a fixed mindset. Instead, figure out how to peel off your wrapper so you can become a flexible thinking "BUBBLE GUM BRAIN!"

  > "Now that you've peeled off your wrapper,
  > Your hope can start to grow.
  > And what you are learning becomes a lot more important
  > Than what you already know."
  >
  > *–Bubble Gum Brain by Julia Cook*

- Teach positive relatable current events each day. This will offset the negative news in our world and create an environment to make kids feel hopeful. There are a lot of good things in our world! CNN's The Good Stuff newsletter is a great resource.

  Teach history and social studies through the lens of improvement. Focus on times when people have worked their way out of dark places while keeping in mind – *"If we forget the past . . . we are condemned to repeat it."*

–George Santayana

- Teach hopeful science (e.g., devastating forest fires clear the path for new growth).
- Find ways for your kids to make a positive difference in the lives of others: volunteering, tutoring or mentoring younger kids, doing service learning projects, etc.
- Add purpose to your classroom by making connections between the content you are teaching and how learning that content can impact the world. Project Based Learning is a great way to guide kids toward researching multiple pathways to problems they want to solve. It also helps to develop personal agency, builds communication skills, and allows kids to understand that they are capable of making an impact.

Joy – It's an Inside Job!

"Making the work become the reward."

–Julia Cook

There is no better feeling in the world than knowing you have made a positive difference in the life of a child. When the "inspired light" in a kid's eyes turns on and you know it's because of you, the feeling is indescribable.

However, the demands placed on educators can at times become overwhelming, and as a result, many amazing teachers are choosing to leave the profession. Teachers today must navigate through ongoing student misbehaviors, academic and standardized testing expectations, long working hours, out of classroom requirements, lack of support, increasing student (and staff) suicidal ideation, and countless other mental health issues.

We are challenged on a daily basis by large class sizes, student inequities, and immigration. On top of all of this, we're expected to help our students build a sense of *hope* for their futures and give them the tools they need to become healthy adults.

When the perfect storm of student and systemic needs creates a mismatch between expectations and realities of our profession, disappointment and defeat often set in. Teachers are doing everything they can to make things work, but when the educator's tidal wave is knocking you off your feet, how do you continue to get back up again? When the system is failing you, how do you keep from feeling like a failure?

The trick? Stop searching for happiness and FIND your JOY!

Finding Joy

Everyone wants to be happy, but happiness is an emotional response to an outcome. You do "A" and then "B" is supposed to happen. But when "B" doesn't happen, it can make you anything *but* happy.

I was always searching for happiness by trying to gain my mom's approval, no matter what it took. One day, I decided to deep clean her house. I remember thinking, "If I do a great job, she'll be so appreciative and happy with me, and then I will happy." I spent about six hours vacuuming, cleaning windows and bathrooms, cleaning underneath furniture, etc.

When I finally finished, she came out of her bedroom and said, "Those are not cleaning towels! Why would you use those to clean? And why are all these cleaners still on the counter? I sure would appreciate it if you cleaned up after yourself! When you take something out . . . put it away!"

This was not the response I was looking for. I felt disappointed, sad, and my happy was sitting on a rocket ship on its way to MARS! I did "A" – and I did it really well – and "B" didn't even come close to happening! The minute my mom saw the disappointment on my face she changed her tune immediately and tried to rectify the situation as best she could, but the damage was done, and I was angry. Looking back, I know my mom's intent was not to hurt me. She was just reacting to her view of the world.

We cannot control how others react, respond, or interpret our actions. That's why happiness cannot be the motivating fuel behind what we do. It can be the icing on the cake, but it cannot be the cake itself.

Joy is a result of inner peace and satisfaction. It's seeing the value in the process as opposed to the response. It's a feeling we have when we are doing what we are cut out to do – no matter what the outcome. Joy is when doing the work becomes the reward. It is always in process, and it is always under construction.

Instead of being angry at my mom for not responding the way I expected her to, I should have focused on the joy of cleaning to help her. The purpose should have been more important to me than her response, which I had no control over.

When Others TRY TO Steal Your Joy

Have you ever worked extremely hard on a proposal, project, or lesson plan, counted on great expectations for its impact, only to have it fail because of circumstances that are out of your control?

Thanks to the digital world we live in, my own joy was completely vaporized a few years back when I discovered I had acquired a group of very vocal "unfans." These "Keyboard Warriors" would flood X and Instagram with 5–10 negative posts a day. They highjacked school Facebook pages that advertised upcoming visits, and blasted I was an ableist, a racist, and a horrible person who hurts kids. They would include snippet examples from various books to promote their opinions.

I take my audience feedback very seriously. When somebody criticizes my books, I use an empathetic lens to view the critique thru their perspective. My goal is to help kids, and when I make mistakes, I own them, learn from them, and fix them.

Over the past 20 years, I have made A LOT of mistakes. For example, the first printing of *I Can't Believe You Said That* featured a character of color named "Bossy Bernice." Some people were offended by that name. "So, you are assuming, Julia Cook, that all girls with brown skin are bossy?" Valid point taken! In the next printing, the book's quality drastically improved because the character was simply renamed "Bernice."

When I realized what was going on, I was shell-shocked! How could anyone think that I would intentionally (or unintentionally) hurt kids? I scoured the internet attempting to find out why this was happening. Maybe if I could talk to these people, they'd realize my intent is only to help. I needed to understand why they wanted to destroy my brand and shred my reputation.

One of the posts contained an extremely valid complaint. In the book *Soda Pop Head*, Lester is teased and looked down upon by his peers when he gets angry and loses his temper.

"There goes Lester
Watch him fester.
His ears start to fizz.
He gets mad as a griz.
His face turns red.
He's a Soda Pop Head.
You just never know
When he's gonna blow.
His cap will go flying,
If it hits you, you'll be crying.
So, you'd better stay away.
From Lester today!"

The post read:

"JULIA COOK SHAMES CHILDREN! You should never shame a child for displaying emotions. This author is toxic and extremely harmful to our kids! All of her books should be banned from schools immediately. She is a horrible example for today's kids!"

Part of this comment is right!

We should never shame kids for how they are feeling. This book needed to change. I peeled myself off of the pavement, wiped the tears out of my eyes, and reworked the story:

> "I am Lester
> Watch me fester.
> My ears start to fizz.
> I get mad as a griz.
> My face turns red.
> I'm a Soda Pop Head.
> I just never know
> When I'm gonna blow.
> My cap will go flying,
> If it hits you, you'll be crying.
> So, you'd better stay away.
> I'm ANGRY today!"

Next, I used every resource I could find to locate the creator of the viral post. I reached out to her through email.

Dear ----------- -

I wanted to reach out and thank you for having the courage to speak out about Soda Pop Head. You are 100% right! Children should never be shamed when showing emotions. I have rewritten the book and the illustrator has changed the images to remove shaming from this story. I am attaching the new version for your review.

I consider all of my books to forever be "works in progress," and my only intent is to help kids. Thank you for helping me make this book better. Your feedback is, and always will be, very valuable.

Sincerely,
Julia Cook

So, I took the high road, thinking my email would reveal my true character, and the negativity would stop.

I could not have been more wrong. Three days later, I received an email reply.

Julia –

Yes, you have changed Soda Pop Head, but the damage from this book and many of your other books has been done. What do you plan to do about the millions of kids you have shamed in the past? What about them?

My head started to spin as I read that email. People are going to think horrible, untrue things about me, and there is nothing I can do about it . . . except quit.

My husband came home from work and found me curled up in a corner on the floor, sobbing uncontrollably, holding the wadded-up email reply in my hand. He took the paper, unfolded it carefully, and read it.

"I can't do it anymore. I try so hard. Why is this happening to me? All I want to do is write books that help kids. Everyone is going to think this stuff is true. No matter what I do or how hard I try, I can't fix this. I don't have anything left inside. I'm so empty. I'm done!"

He wrapped his arms tightly around me and let me cry it out. Then he said, "YOU are NOT AWFUL". Juli, people love your books, and they love you! Think of how many kids out there that you have helped . . . probably millions! Everyone who has met you knows firsthand that this is bullshit! You're Julia Cook! You wrote *Bully Beans*. Are you seriously going to cave and let these ignorant a-holes bully you online? Quit hanging out with Vic and Tim (AKA "victim") and keep doing "YOU." These people can only steal your joy if you let them.

After that day, I unplugged from X and stopped actively searching online for my unfans. The negative posts continued, but after a while, schools caught on and started to delete them. My own millennial children congratulated me on being famous enough to have online trolls (go figure!). Thousands of school counselors and teachers rallied with posts of their own in an attempt to stand up to the "Keyboard Warriors" on my behalf.

This experience, although brutally painful to endure, has helped me realize in order to have joy when I am at work, I need to believe what I am doing is meaningful. The massive support I have received through all of this from my family, friends, and fans has helped me strengthen this belief.

If online bullying affected me this severely, imagine how devastating it can be for kids, who may not have amazing support systems in place. Many young adults find themselves forced into combatting complex issues with underdeveloped problem-solving skills, as they question who they are and whom they are expected to become.

I have also changed my outlook. Instead of being angry at my unfans, I actually feel sorry for them. They must have a good reason for being so unkind. Maybe someone vaporized their joy, and they are trying everything they can think of to get it back.

Never again will I allow myself to be heartbroken, upset, and depleted by the actions of those I cannot control. I now choose to focus on the process of doing everything I can to make a positive difference in the lives of kids. And guess what? I'm back to enJOYing my job!

Focus on What You Can Control

There are so many factors impacting education today that are out of our control. Attendance, parent and administrative support, class size, salary, student home life, etc. In order to make an impact, we need to focus on the things that we do have control over, and our JOY happens to be one of those things.

> Note: I did not list misbehaviors under factors we cannot control. Every misbehavior is a result of an unmet need. If we can stop focusing so much on the behaviors we are seeing and strategically figure out what the unmet needs are, many misbehaviors will decrease – so that one, in part, is under our control.

Many people lump joy and happiness together because they both make us feel good on the inside, but in reality, there are many differences between the two. What follows is a random selection of my favorite universal observations.

- **Happiness** is external and depends upon the reactions and responses others have to our actions. **Joy** is internal. It is independent of the circumstances of others.
- **Happiness** is an emotional response. **Joy** is an act of will.
- **Happiness** is "having what you want." **Joy** is "wanting what you have."
- **Happiness** is stimulus driven (similar to an addiction). To maintain your level of happiness, the stimulus must continually increase. Every time we attain happiness, we raise the bar: I finally have a Mercedes . . . now I want a Lamborghini. We never seem to get enough. **Joy** is feelings of inner contentment, and is ongoing.
- **Happiness** is a result. **Joy** is a cause and a foundation.
- **Happiness** is extremely inconsistent and out of your control. **Joy** is very consistent and is in your total control.

- **Happiness** is cosmetic. **Joy** is character.
- **Happiness** meets your surface needs. **Joy** meets your deepest needs.
- **Happiness**, like a thermometer, registers conditions. **Joy**, like a thermostat, controls conditions.
- **Happiness** is a mile wide and an inch deep. **Joy** is a mile high and a mile deep.

And finally,

- **Happiness** evaporates in suffering. **Joy** intensifies in suffering.

The Candle Problem

In the 1930s, Gestalt psychologist Karl Dunker developed a unique experiment called "The Candle Problem," which Dan Pink presented in a TED Talk called "The Puzzle of Motivation."[1]

The Candle Problem is a cognitive performance test that measures functional fixedness as it relates to performance. Functional fixedness refers to the bias that limits people to use objects only in the way they are traditionally used.

People were divided into two groups: A and B. Each group was given a small cardboard box full of tacks, a candlestick, and a book of matches.

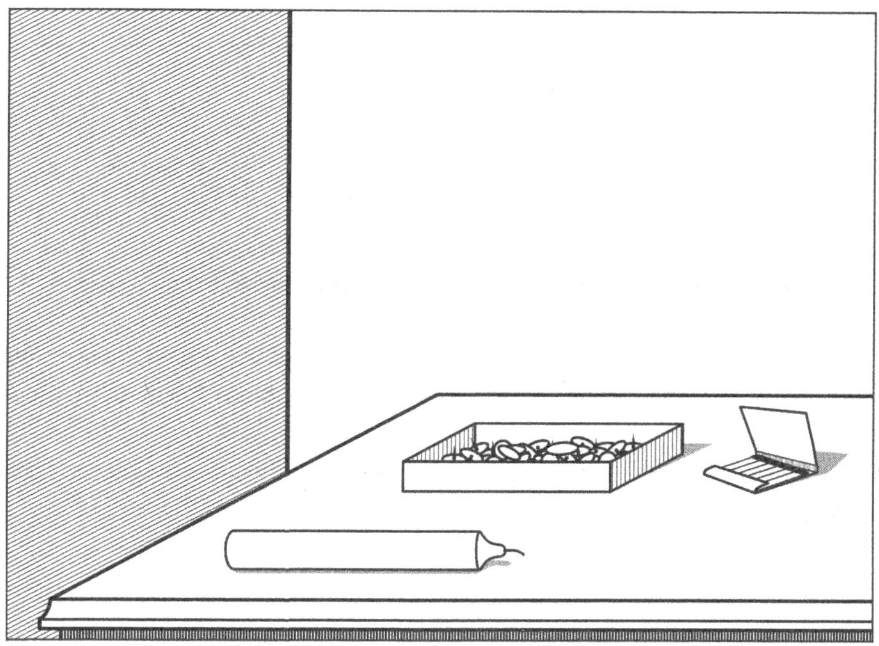

The members of group A were told by Dr. Dunker that he and his team were interested in simply observing them as they solved the problem and would collect norms on the times needed to complete the task. Group B was told that if they solved the problem quickly enough, they would be given money.

To solve the problem, the candle must be lit, attached to the wall, and no wax can drop on the table below. Many creative attempts were made including tacking the candle to the wall, melting some of the candle wax and using it as adhesive to stick the candle on the side of the wall. None of these were successful.

This is the solution to The Candle Problem:

Through thousands of trials with the tacks starting out inside the box, group A participants would end up solving The Candle Problem faster than those in group B.

However, when the materials were presented to the groups with the tacks outside of the box like this . . .

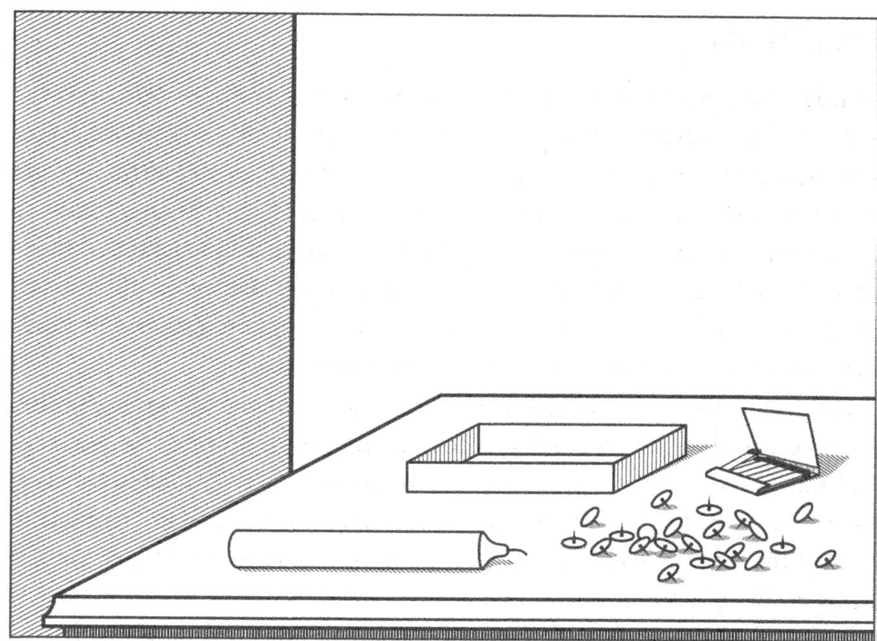

Both groups A and B consecutively solved the problem much quicker and within the same time frame.

Dunker's conclusion: When faced with completing a simple mechanical task or solving a problem that does not involve complex thinking strategies, monetary rewards will increase performance levels. However, when tackling a more complex task that requires creative thinking and problem-solving, monetary rewards decrease overall performance. This happens because more thinking energy is placed on what we will receive when we complete the task than simply figuring out how to complete it.

The point is, if our happiness depends on the actions and responses of others, and the students we deal with are in crisis, attaining and achieving happiness can be a huge challenge.

It's obvious that the challenges kids are facing today are very complex. To tackle these challenges effectively, we must think both cognitively and creatively and focus on our energy and resources. If we teach kids for a paycheck or a test performance score, we lose our creativity, our zest, and our effectiveness. To make the biggest impact, we need to pay more attention to the process as opposed to the product. It's the process that contains the value – and rewards, both intrinsic and monetary, will always chase value!

Joyful Rigor

In the book *The Smartest Kids in the World*, author Amanda Ripley compares the underachieving education system of the United States with the education system superpowers of the world.[2] Ripley placed US students in study abroad homes and had them attend schools in Finland, Poland, and South Korea. In an attempt to figure out what we are missing, she studied what parents and teachers of these countries did differently from those in the United States. Ripley concluded that one of the secrets to achieving record high levels of student performance is experiencing "Joyful Rigor" in the classroom multiple times a day.

Joyful Rigor occurs when kids are given high expectations and are supported through the process of meeting those expectations by teachers who create engaging, relatable, and stimulating learning environments. In a nutshell, when kids genuinely enjoy the learning experience, see relevance in the content, feel secure and supported, and are expected to do great things, achievement soars. Make it engaging and they will learn!

A few years ago, I did an online search "How to find JOY in the workplace," and Mark Sanborn's book *The Fred Factor* popped up as recommended reading.

As educators, finding our own personal joy in the workplace can at times be very difficult. *The Fred Factor,* a motivational story about Sanborn's mailman, spotlights the process of learning to enjoy work. Fred loves being a mailman. He has creatively turned an ordinary job into a joyful, extraordinary career by building meaningful relationships with his route members. He goes above and beyond every day to create value for others without spending money. Fred considers it a great pleasure to take care of the mail he delivers and the people he delivers it to. Instead of delivering mail to people, he delivers "people" their mail.[3]

Using Fred as an example of process over product, Sanborn explains that everyone makes a difference. We each have the power to choose to be exceptional, regardless of the circumstances we are in. Insignificant and ordinary jobs cease to exist when they are performed by extraordinary people. Nobody can prevent you from becoming exceptional at what you do.

When Fred goes out of his way to make the lives of others more enjoyable through actions he can control, his own joy grows. Fred's efforts become noticed and appreciated by all, making him feel more significant. It's not what he does that matters, it's how he makes others feel by doing it.

---

[2]Ripley, Amanda, *The Smartest Kids in the World*, Simon & Schuster Paperbacks, New York, 2013.
[3]Sanborn, Mark, *The Fred Factor: How Passion in Your Work and Life Can Turn the Ordinary into the Extraordinary*, Crown Currency, 2004.

We can easily relate these concepts to teaching. How can we expect our students to become engaged and involved in class if we do not do the same? How can we expect our kids to become exceptional if we cannot model the process?

Actively finding our joy will not solve every problem that we encounter, but it may be the little boost we need to put our problem-solving strategies in motion. JOY can be the "sparkler" that gets us moving in a better direction. Regardless of the circumstances, we can choose to become exceptional, and nobody can prevent us from doing so.

Have you ever noticed that the majority of the word "enjoy" comes from JOY itself? Think about it!

Worth Remembering

- **Happiness** – An emotional response to an outcome. It's a means to an end. Depends on reactions of others. Every time we attain happiness, we raise the bar. We never seem to get enough.
- **Joy** – When doing the work becomes the reward. It's always in process. Joy is always under construction.

Happiness	vs	Joy
External		Internal
Dependent on circumstances		Independent of circumstances
Emotional response		Act of will
Having what you want		Wanting what you have
External euphoria		Inner contentment
Effect		Cause
Result		Foundation
Inconsistent		Consistent
Temporary		Eternal
Cosmetic		Character
From outside circumstances		From within
Meets surface needs		Meets deepest needs
Thermometer – registers conditions		Thermostat – regulates conditions
Evaporates in suffering		Intensifies in suffering

- To remain motivated in all that we do, we all need to feel like we matter.
- You may feel helpless at times because you can't solve the problem. But by finding your joy, YOU can be the person who puts the problem-solving in motion.

Worth Trying

In her book *Joy! You Find What You Look For*, author Gina Prosch suggests the following strategies to maintain joy in your daily life.[4]

- **Encourage Gratitude** – Gratitude is the doorway to joy.
- **Do Daily Reflections** – Write down or talk about every day's joy.
- **Point Out the Positives** – Don't allow the daily negatives to overshadow the positives.
- **Do a Positive Reframe** – We must experience uncomfortable to learn.
- **Start Small** – Start with the little joys and build from there.
- **Encourage Healthy Habits** – It's hard to feel joy when you don't feel well.
- **Frontload Joy** – Make it a priority to do something you enjoy every single day.

[4]Prosch, Gina, *Joy! You Find What You Look For*, Boys Town Press, Omaha, NE, 2023.

The Power of Concrete Visuals

06

"In order to teach children, you must enter their view of the world."

–Julia Cook

My first memorable experience with a concrete visual happened when I was 5 or 6. I had a really bad habit of interrupting. Words would pop into my head, slide down onto my tongue . . . and out of my mouth they would come! My babysitter Blanche was attempting to watch *Heartbeat of a Volcano* (a sought-after documentary that aired in the 1970s), with me in the same room.

"Can I make a volcano at your house? You should see the volcano we made at school!"

"Shhhh . . . I really want to hear this part."

"We used cardboard and a paper towel tube. Then we dipped newspaper strips in this sticky glue stuff. Then. . ."

"Just a minute, Juli. I want to hear this part."

"But we painted it brown and used baking soda and put food coloring in some vinegar and . . ."

"Juli, you interrupt so much, I think your mouth is a volcano!"

That comment stopped me in my tracks.

I remember running over to a mirror and looking inside of my mouth. That made perfect sense to me. My mouth was a volcano, my words were the lava, and it wasn't my fault that I erupted (interrupted). Everyone knows that volcanos can't control their lava!

(Continued)

Years later, when a teacher asked me to do a lesson on interrupting, it triggered that memory in my mind, and to make my lesson more meaningful, I crafted that concrete visual into a story: *My Mouth is a Volcano!* I had no idea at the time that my little story would eventually evolve into a best-selling children's book that everyone can relate to. However, this goes to show how incredibly powerful a good concrete visual can be.

Examining with Your Senses

"If you can examine something with your senses, it's concrete," Chip and Dan Heath write in their best-selling book *Made to Stick*. "Concrete language helps people, especially novices, understand new concepts."[1] We all know that learning

---

[1] Heath, Chip, and Dan Heath, *Made to Stick*, Random House, New York, 2008, p. 104.

can be extremely difficult sometimes. I have found that in order for most kids to thoroughly gain an understanding of a concept, they must experience *the ITs*:

SEE "IT."
HEAR "IT."
FEEL "IT."
DO "IT."
DEMONSTRATE "IT" TO SOMEBODY ELSE.
And
RELATE "IT" TO SOMETHING THEY ALREADY KNOW.

Using concrete visuals is a great way to make this process fun and much more doable.

Concrete Visual Activities

In 2024, I launched a resource website (Cookiebytesbyjulia.com) that includes demonstration videos of an ever-growing collection of concrete visual ideas.

Here are 10 of my favorites.

#1 Listening and Talking – A One-Way Street!

PURPOSE:

This visual demonstrates why we cannot talk and listen at the same time.

MATERIALS NEEDED:

- 2 small Matchbox cars
- 1 piece of toy racetrack (approx. 12" long)

DIRECTIONS:

Place one end of the racetrack just below your lower lip. Explain: "Let's pretend we all have a racetrack that is sitting on our tongue, going all the way back to our brain and coming out of our mouth.

"Every time you say something or make any kind of a sound, a little tiny car drives out of your mouth on that track." (Place one car on the track as if it is coming out of your mouth.)

"Every time someone says something to you, another little car drives into your brain on that same track." (Place another car on the track as if it is coming into your mouth on the other end of the track.)

"So if you talk or make a sound when somebody is talking to you, what happens to the cars? They crash! (Crash the cars on the track.)

"Conclusion: You cannot talk or make noise and listen at the same time because the words crash outside of your head and nothing gets in."

#2 "ALL IN" Listening – Be the Quicker Picker-Upper!

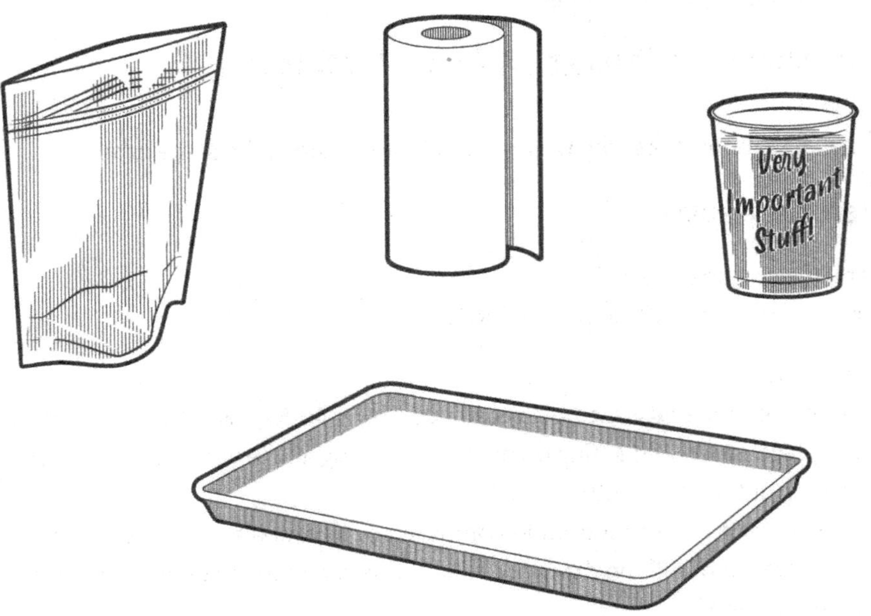

PURPOSE:

This visual demonstrates active listening and gives kids answers to two very important kid questions:

Why should I do _______?

and

What's in it for me when I do it?

MATERIALS NEEDED:

- Paper Towels
- Clear Plastic Gallon Bag
- Clear Plastic Cup labeled "Very Important Stuff!" filled with colored water (RED)
- Tray or Pan

DIRECTIONS:

Teachers always say, "LISTEN" "I NEED YOU TO LISTEN" "I DON'T THINK YOU'RE LISTENING."

We definitely overuse the word *listen*. Try this instead.

"OKAY I need you *ALL IN*."

"ALL IN means your eyes are on me, your mouths are quiet and your ears are as big as your palms." (Hold your palms up in front of your ears showing how big they need to be.)

"When you are ALL IN everything I say goes into your head, and you don't miss anything. I have a lot of important information that I want you to know." (Pour some of the water out into the pan.)

"If you are ALL IN, you can be the QUICKER PICKER-UPPER!" (Soak up all of the colored water into the paper towel.)

"Look it's in your head . . . all of it. But if you are talking when I talk (pour more water into the pan) it's kinda like you are trying to soak it up with this plastic bag. (Try soaking up the water with the plastic bag.) Look! Nothing gets in."

Hold up the soaked paper towel. "Once information is in your brain, do you ever have to put it in there again? No, it's in there! All you need to do is find it. But if you are talking when I'm talking to you, you're probably going to have to find time later to soak in my very important stuff, and that could cut into your free time."

This exercise gives kids answers to their very important questions:

Why should I do _________?

and

What's in it for me when I do it?

#3 Chunk It!

PURPOSE:

This visual demonstrates the bounce-back superpower tool of breaking big problems down into smaller ones.

MATERIALS NEEDED:

- Large cake mixing bowl
- 1 family-size box of Lucky Charms (or other kid-loved cereal)
- Large serving spoon
- Small cereal bowl
- Teaspoon

DIRECTIONS:

Ask your students, "Who loves Lucky Charms?"

Invite one of the kids who raises their hand to come to the front of the class and face the kids.

"You love Lucky Charms so much, that I'm going to give you a bowl of them!"

Hand your student the big cake bowl and empty the entire box into to. Then, hand them a serving spoon.

"Here is your bowl! Eat it . . . eat it all." Then: "Can you do it?"

"No!"

"Why not?"

"Because it's too much, and it will make me sick."

Grab the small bowl and scoop some of the cereal into it with the smaller spoon on top.

"Well, if I give you a small bowl of Lucky Charms, can you eat all of it?"

"Yes."

"Then if you wait a little while can you eat another bowl?"

"Yes."

"That's because your stomach can digest a small bowl, but this big bowl is way too much at one time. That's like a big problem. Your brain cannot digest a great big problem all at once. But if you break down your big problem into smaller chunks, your brain can digest it. Always remember, a big problem is just a bunch of little problems stuck together."

"The same goes for a big assignment. Break down your big assignment into smaller chunks that your brain can digest instead of trying to do it all at once."

#4 Addiction/Habit String

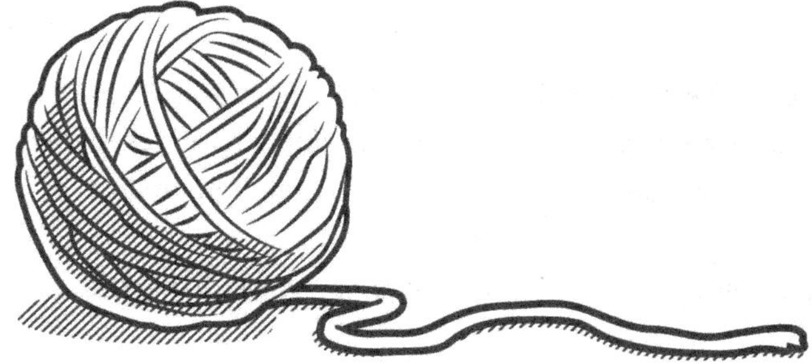

This is a great lesson that works for any number of addictions and bad habits, originated by Tom Jackson, and found in his book *Activities That Teach*.[2]

---

[2]Jackson, Tom, *Activities That Teach*, Redrock Publishing, 1993.

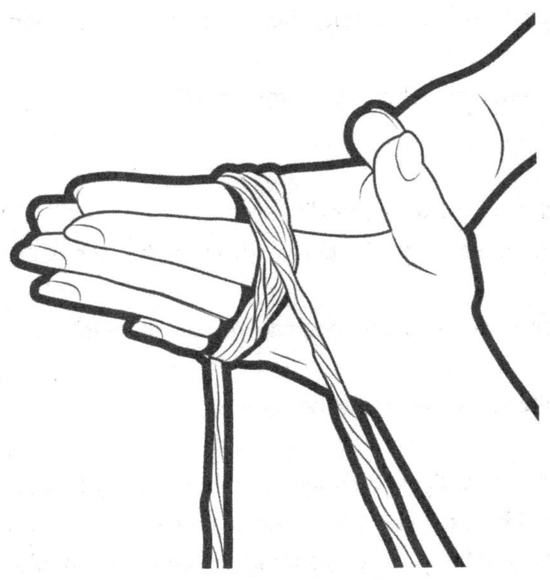

PURPOSE:
This visual demonstrates the forming of habits both good and bad.

MATERIALS NEEDED:

• Piece of yarn or string (5–10 feet long)

DIRECTIONS:
Ask one student to come to the front of the class and place his palms together with his thumbs pointing up. Wrap the string around the student's hands as follows:

"If I wrap this string around your hands once can you pull them apart?"
"Yes."
"If I wrap this string around your hands three times, can you pull them apart?"
"Yes."
"If I wrap this string around your hands 27 times can you pull them apart?"
"No."
"That's like a habit or an addiction."
Wrap the string around their hands as you say:

"If you try vaping once, can you quit?"

"Yes."

"If you try vaping three times can you quit?"

"Yes."

"If you try vaping 27 times can you quit?"

"No, probably not."

"Since you're a kid, you can't buy vape juice at a vape store, so you have to get it on the street. Sometimes, people put chemicals in street vape juice that wraps you up 27 times the first time you try it. Knowing this now, what is the best choice for you?"

"Don't ever even try it."

"Yep!"

#5 Spread Too Thin

PURPOSE:

This visual allows the teacher to convey an authentic understanding for being stressed out and over-obligated.

MATERIALS NEEDED:

- 1 piece of bread
- Jam or jelly
- 4 plastic knives labeled "FAMILY," "SCHOOL," "FRIENDS," and "ACTIVITIES"

DIRECTIONS:

Place a small amount of jam or jelly (3/4 tsp) in the middle of the bread and use the knives accordingly to spread it around as you say: "This piece of bread is life and you are the jam. You have a lot going on. You have family commitments—going to visit your grandparents, family holiday gatherings, hanging out with your cousins (spread the jam with the family knife)."

"You've got a lot of things you need to do for school—assignments that are due, projects to work on, tests to get ready for (spread the jam with the school knife)."

"You have friends that you want to hang out with and do things with (spread the jam with the friend's knife)."

"And, you have so many activities that you enjoy doing—soccer, music lessons, Taekwondo, etc. (spread the jam with the activities knife)."

Do you ever feel like there isn't enough of you to go around? Do you ever get spread so thin that it feels like you are accidentally poking holes in your bread?

BUTTER
BUTTER

PURPOSE:

This concrete visual teaches and helps kids better understand the concept of teamwork.

MATERIALS NEEDED:

- Baking sheet
- 2 cups of flour
- 1 tsp salt
- Bag of chocolate chips
- Sugar
- Brown sugar
- Baking soda
- Eggs
- Picture of an oven
- Mixing bowl
- Measuring spoons
- Stirring spoon
- Egg beater
- And anything else needed to make chocolate chip cookies

DIRECTIONS:

Hold up items as you say:

"If you want to make chocolate chip cookies, you need all of these things. You need an oven, a mixing bowl, measuring spoons, a big spoon, eggs, sugar, chips, baking soda, etc. But check this out: you need 2 cups of flour and only 1 teaspoon of salt."

"Does that mean the flour is more important than the salt? No, because it's not about the salt or the flour. It's about what they contribute and how they work together with the other ingredients to make the cookie. Every ingredient has a role, and EVERY ROLE MATTERS!"

"That's just like a team! Every team member has a role, and EVERY ROLE MATTERS."

#7 Playing Cards

PURPOSE:

This concrete visual teaches kids to strategically use their individual strengths.

MATERIALS NEEDED:

- Over-sized playing cards
- 3–5 Traditional decks of playing cards – all different styles/colors – typical, holiday, animals, etc.
- Mini playing cards
- Teeny tiny playing cards
- Waterproof playing cards
- Gold playing cards (https://www.walmart.com/ip/Bicycle-Aureo-Gold-Playing-Cards/610173231)

DIRECTIONS:

Pass out decks of cards to various students. Ask the kids with card decks to line up at the front of the classroom, facing the other students, and remove one card from their deck.

"Look at all of these cool cards! Each of them has a unique quality. The big cards can help people see the numbers better. Maybe you want to play cards in a swimming pool or a hot tub, and these are perfect for that. You might only have a small table, so using these mini cards would work really well for that. If you're feeling exotic, you could use your gold cards. If you love (dogs) you might want to play with this deck. If you just want to play regular cards, these are perfect!"

Now let me ask you a question. If you're playing a card game, will you win more games with:

- Your gold cards or your big cards?
- Your mini cards or your dog cards?
- Your waterproof cards or your regular cards?

"You're right! It doesn't matter. You see, winning card games is kinda like winning at life. We are all made up of 52 cards and 2 jokers, but when it comes to winning at life, it doesn't matter how big you are. It doesn't matter how cute you are. It doesn't matter how rich you are. . . . When it comes to winning at life, it's all about how you play your cards, NOT what the cards look like."

#8 Cross the Line!

PURPOSE:
This concrete visual helps kids understand the effects of peer pressure.

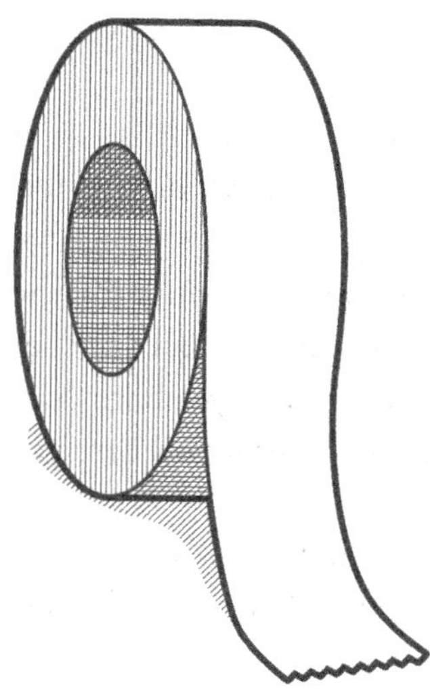

MATERIALS:

- Piece of masking tape 3–5 feet long
- 3–5 kids

DIRECTIONS:

Place the tape on the floor making a straight line. Ask the kids to gather on one side of the line and face you with the line in between.

Say: "This line represents a choice (stealing, cheating, underage drinking, vaping, etc.) Today, we will say it stands for vaping. If you cross the line, you vape."

Ask one student to stand directly opposite you and have the other kids stand next to and behind that student.

"Here's a scenario. You are at a party and you have never really thought about vaping before. I'm at the party and you think I'm one of the super cool kids. I start talking to you and I invite you to try vaping. Before you know it, I pull you across this line and you try it." (Grab a hold of the students' hands and pull them over the line.)

"Here's another scenario. You are at a party and you have talked with your parents and others in the past about the dangers of vaping. You have made up your mind that vaping is not for you. I take your hands and try to pull you across this line and you pull back resisting me." (Student pulls back resisting as you try to pull them across the line.)

"Here is a third scenario. You are at a party with your friends. You choose pretty good friends who are known for making great decisions. When I try to convince you to vape (attempt to pull student across the line), your friends grab a hold of you and help pull you away from the line. (Kids go on each side of the student, take a hold of the student's arms, belt, waist, etc., and pull back, keeping the kid from crossing.) There is no way I'm going to be able to convince you to try vaping. The force to not do it is too strong."

"Here is a fourth scenario. You are at a party and you view yourself as a great decision-maker. You have decided no matter what, vaping is not for you. You feel you are strong enough to hang out with anyone because you are convinced that others will not sway your decision-making skills. I try to pull you across the line convincing you to vape (attempt to pull kid across) and resist me, but your so-called friends start to push you toward the line as opposed to keep you back. (Kids on the sides collectively push the student over the line.) No matter how hard you try to resist, you end up crossing the line."

"THE POINT TO ALL OF THIS: WHO YOU HANG OUT WITH WILL ULTI-MATELY INFLUENCE THE DECISIONS YOU MAKE. Be friendly to everyone, but be mindful of those you decide to call your friends."

9 My Self-Worth – Your Self-Worth

PURPOSE:

The purpose of this visual is to help kids understand that when they say and do things that are unkind to others, they end up hurting themselves twice as much as the person they are unkind to.

MATERIALS NEEDED:

- Two Styrofoam cups
- Clear pitcher full of colored water labeled "SELF-WORTH"
- Permanent Marker
- Hairpin, or something similar
- Cake pan or tray

DIRECTIONS:

Using the marker, label the cups "MY SELF-WORTH" and "YOUR SELF-WORTH."

"Let's say that the water in this pitcher is full of SELF-WORTH." (Fill each cup with Self-Worth water and place the cups next to each other inside the cake pan or on the tray with the words showing.)

"When you say or do something unkind to another person, your unkindness comes from you and pokes a hole in that person's self-worth." (Using the hairpin, poke a hole from inside of the My SELF-WORTH cup through the outside of the Your SELF-WORTH cup.)

"Then when you're done being unkind, you have to pull pretty hard to take the hole puncher out, and you end up accidentally poking a second hole on the back side of the Your SELF-WORTH cup. This drains your SELF-WORTH twice as fast as the person you were unkind to." (Pull the hairpin out of the two cups and put a hole in the opposite side of the My Self-Worth cup before taking the pin out of the cup. The My Self-Worth cup should have 2 holes in it and should be losing twice as much self-worth as the Your Self-Worth cup.)

"THE POINT: When you hurt others, you end up hurting yourself twice as much."

#10 Emotional Control in the Bag

PURPOSE:

This visual helps kids understand what emotions do, and why it is so important to learn how to control them.

MATERIALS NEEDED:

- 4 balls (3"–4" in diameter): blue, green, orange, red
- Mesh net bag that balls will easily fit inside of
- 4 round balloons slightly inflated (5"–6" in diameter): blue, green, orange, red
- 1 balloon not inflated: (green, orange, or blue)

DIRECTIONS:

Place all four balls on a table, pick up the mesh net bag, and explain the following while you put the balls into the net one by one:

"We all have 4 basic human emotions:

Joy (hold up red ball and place it into the bag) *makes us feel good on the inside.*

Sadness (hold up blue ball and place it into the bag) *helps us get through things that are hard.*

Anger (hold up orange ball and place it into the bag) *protects us, gives us a place to put negative feelings, and helps us understand that this might be a better way to deal with our situation.*

and

Anxiety (hold up green ball and place it into the bag) *helps us prepare for things that might happen so we can be ready for them."*

"As long as our emotions fit inside of us, things are good, but sometimes our emotions start to grow."

Take balls out of bag and replace them with the balloons.

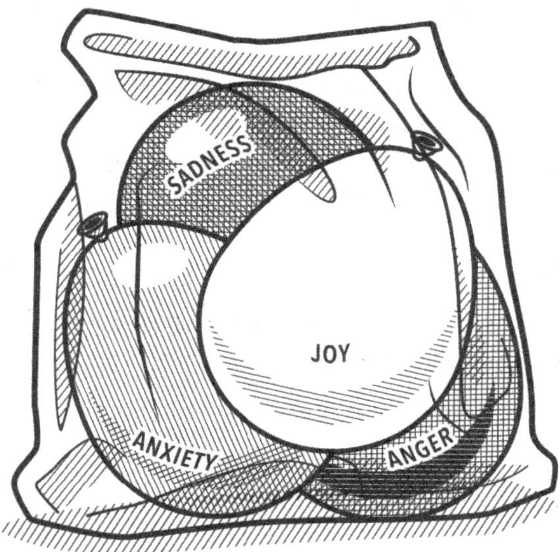

Blow up one uninflated balloon (blue, orange, or green) until it is larger than the bag (almost overinflated), and squeeze the mouthpiece or neck so the air won't come out.

"Sometimes, our emotions get SO big that they don't fit inside of us at all."

Demonstrate trying to unsuccessfully stuff the overinflated balloon inside of the bag.

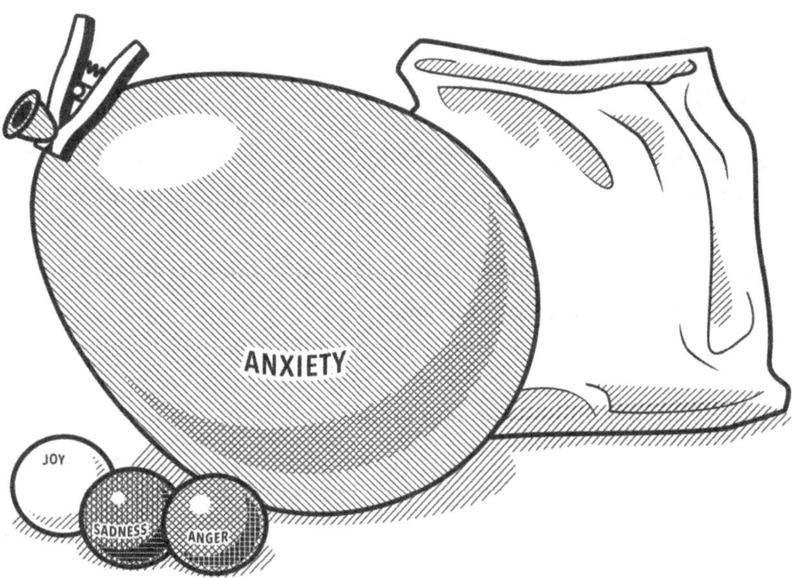

"It's okay if your emotions get big sometimes. That's what they are supposed to do. The trick is to find creative ways to shrink them back down and control their size."

Pull on both sides of the neck and make a squeaky sound as you let a tiny bit of air out of the balloon.

"If you can't figure out how to be in control of your emotions, that air will eventually come out, and you never know where they're going to land!"

Let go of the balloon, and watch it spin through the air as it deflates.

Worth Remembering

- Learning can be extremely difficult sometimes. To thoroughly gain an understanding of a concept, kids must experience the "IT's."

    SEE "IT."

    HEAR "IT."

    FEEL "IT."

    DO "IT."

    DEMONSTRATE "IT" TO SOMEBODY ELSE.

    and

    RELATE "IT" TO SOMETHING THEY ALREADY KNOW.

- Using concrete visuals promotes active learning.
- Using concrete visuals helps kids relate content to their view of the world.
- Using concrete visuals makes your classroom more interesting, engaging, and fun.

Worth Trying

- Take a stroll through a hardware store, grocery store, or discount store and look for objects that you can use to create your own concrete visuals. Let your creativity run wild!
- Try any of the concrete visuals in this chapter as is, or feel free to adapt them to work for other teaching concepts and ideas.

Unlearning Helplessness – Motivating the Underachiever

"It usually takes at least one person who knows what to do and how and is willing to go all the way with an underachieving person to reverse their underachievement."

–Asuni Lady Zeal

A few years ago, I was asked to help teach a unique writing workshop for a select group of struggling high school students. The school bussed 56 students (grades 9–12) to a beautiful animal rescue/sanctuary. The goal of the workshop was to have the kids observe the animals and read about their struggles to survive and how they ended up at the sanctuary. Then, they were asked to choose an animal and write about how their own struggles in life compared.

Shawn, a highly energetic, tiny-framed 9th grader with a bleached blonde buzz cut and a smile that melted my heart, had not written down a single word before lunch. He also made it very clear that he did not identify with the struggles of any of the sanctuary residents, and he did not shy away from telling everyone, "This assignment and this whole day is a stupid waste of my time!"

Shawn appeared to be very bright, but after visiting with his English teacher at the workshop, I found out that he literally had not picked up a pencil at school or turned in a single assignment since 7th grade. He went from being an honor roll student to failing every class, not because he wasn't capable, but because he absolutely refused to do his work.

"Our district keeps promoting him due to *system logistics*," his teacher told me, "So he really doesn't see the need to have to do anything. He has a rough home life, and he's not the easiest kid to have in class. He does fine for me behaviorally, but

(*Continued*)

other teachers really struggle with him. I thought this experience might make a difference."

"Hey Shawn," I said after lunch, "I'd love to read your story."

"I'm not writing one."

"Why?"

"Because you don't want to read what I would write."

"Really? Tell me all about what you would write."

"I absolutely, positively HATE school, and everything about it . . . well almost."

"Why?"

"Because every teacher I have makes me feel like a worthless piece of shit . . . except her."

"Your English teacher?"

"Yep . . . she gets me. I like her and I like going to her class, but the rest of my teachers suck."

"What do they do that makes you feel this way?"

Shawn started rattling off numerous situations by class period. I let him vent as I jotted down the bones of what he was saying on a piece of scratch paper. His negative rant lasted about 15 minutes. When he was done, I showed him my notes.

"Look! Here's your story!"

"I can't write that stuff down! I'll get in trouble! Besides, nobody will believe me."

"Is all of this true?"

"It's true to me!"

"Okay, I have an idea. Instead of writing down what your teachers do wrong, why don't you write about what you would do right if you were the teacher. Take one school day and write down how things should be instead of how they are."

"Okay, I guess I can do that."

Shawn grabbed my scratch paper, his notepad, and a pen, walked over to a quiet corner in the room, sat down, and started writing. A few minutes later, one of his friends came over and humorously harassed him, trying to pull him off task.

"Leave me alone! I'm writing!"

"You're what? You never do your work. Let's go back outside."

"No. I want to get this done! Leave me alone!"

Shawn's English teacher couldn't believe what she was seeing.

"Oh my gosh!" she said. "It's working!"

About 40 minutes later, Shawn stood up with his story in his hand. I walked over to him, and his teacher followed me.

"I'm done! I did it!" he said.

"Can I read it?"

"Nope . . . but I'll read it to you."

What happened next was a big surprise to me. Shawn's story was his raw perception, written with a strong writing skill set and more mature insight than I had ever expected.

Why I Hate School

–by Shawn

When I was little, I loved going to school. My teachers made me feel like I was worth something. I loved everything about it. Now, I absolutely hate going to school. Mostly because it's a huge waste of my time.

Most of my teachers hate me. I can see it in their eyes. A few of my them dislike me so much that they ignore my presence. To them, I am invisible, so why even be there?

(Continued)

There is one exception to this. My English teacher is bomb! She smiles at me every morning. If I'm having a bad day, she senses it and gives me my space. I've let her see what I don't share with other teachers. I show her that I'm really smart, because she deserves to know. I look forward to seeing her every day because I know she cares about me as a person. She always tells us that we are important to her, and she knows how to back up her words with actions.

In a perfect world, all teachers would be like that, but my world is far from perfect.

If I was my math teacher, I would try to make math real so my students could see the purpose in learning it. I wouldn't tell kids, "Mathematics is everywhere you look," and then not show them where to find it. I wouldn't write the assignment on the board, do a few examples out of the book, and then say, "Now get this done and no talking." And I wouldn't pull out my phone and read stuff online when I should be helping my students. If kids can't be on their phones in class, why can teachers be on theirs? If I truly didn't like my job, I would quit, because my students would be able to tell and they deserve a teacher who wants to be there.

If I was my science teacher, I would check my stress at the door instead of taking it out on my students and stressing them out. I also would not bring my personal problems like getting divorced into my classroom. What does that have to do with biology anyway? I also would not destroy curiosity when my students ask questions and act like they are putting me out. I would think about how much courage it takes for a kid to ask a question and never make them feel stupid for doing so. I would help them figure stuff out when they didn't understand and let them know that asking questions is always okay.

If I was my Spanish teacher, I would figure out different ways to teach my students because everyone learns differently. I would also give my students time to work and practice speaking to each other in small groups. By the way, my uncle has Babbel on his computer, and when I go over to his house, he lets me use it. I have taught myself to speak fluent Spanish, but you'll never know that. You treat me like I'm a stupid underachiever.

You never call on me because you don't believe I have anything to offer, so I will take the easy way out and live up to your unexpectations!

If I was my gym teacher, I would give kids the grades they deserve. Being a jock, or having boobs and cute long hair, should not constitute an automatic A. I would give my students grades earned by progress of where they were when they started PE class and how much they have improved by the end. Also, I would never laugh at my students. Instead, I would laugh with them.

If I was my history teacher, I would figure out that everyone isn't excited about studying what happened a long time ago. I would realize that kids don't think about the past. They think about now, so history already has two strikes against itself. I would try a lot harder to relate what happened years ago to what's going on today, so kids get it. I would also understand that if one of my students falls asleep in class, there might be a good reason. Maybe they are bored, or maybe they had to sleep in a car because they got evicted and it's hard to sleep when you're cold.

I could go on and on . . . and on! Something needs to change! But the sad thing about all of this is, no matter what I write . . . nothing's going to change, so why bother.

I stood there speechless for what seemed like an eternity. I looked at Shawn and said the only word that came to me: "WOW!"

"Way to put your feelings down on paper Shawn," his teacher said. "I knew you could write!"

Shawn smiled, handed his story to me, and walked outside.

"Is that all true?" I asked. "Do you think his teachers are really like that?"

"I doubt it," she replied. "But true or not, it's what he sees and believes, and that's the problem."

"Does Shawn play a lot of video games by chance?"

"All Shawn does is play video games. They engulf his whole identity."

A Failing System

My experience that day with Shawn set off an array of emotions. I was encouraged that we got him to write. I appreciated that he trusted me enough to become transparent. I felt empathy for both Shawn and his teachers (there are two sides to every pancake). But most of all I felt sad because the system in place was failing this kid.

I asked Shawn's teacher the video game question because many kids that game a lot appear to lack the effort and motivation needed to win in real life. They simply unlearn how to try hard. Some gamers become conditioned to the instant gratification "push a button-get a point" mentality. Winning a video game can often be much quicker and easier than accomplishing a task in real life. Excessive gaming causes some kids to shut down or quit when the real-life task at hand appears difficult.

According to veteran educator Bob Sullo, there are five things every person needs to achieve[1]:

1. You need to be competent in your abilities

2. You need to have the power to make choices

3. You need to have fun and enjoy the experience

4. You need to feel connected, both to the content and to others involved

5. You must feel safe in your environment.

From Shawn's perspective, it is easy to understand why he is underachieving, as many of these five factors appear to be missing. Throw excessive video gaming into the mix, and every deficit becomes amplified.

Underachieving students have a significant gap between their abilities and what they achieve in school. When academic performance does not reflect potential, underachieving students ultimately pay the price.

Types of Underachievers

Research indicates that nearly 50% of today's school-age children are underachievers.[2] To tackle this issue, we need to first identify the six types of underachievers and then focus on underlying reasons that are causing our kids to underperform.

There are six types of underachievers:

#1 My Way or the Highway Underachiever

This type of underachiever may be stifled from seeing the situation from another point of view. They tend to do just enough to get by and rarely perform to their potential. They do not see the benefit of exerting more effort. In Plato's cave allegory, people are sitting on chairs in a cave, chained to look straight ahead at the wall in front

---

[1]Sullo, Bob, *Activating the Desire to Learn*, Association for Supervision and Curriculum Development (ASCD), Alexandria, Virginia, 2007.

[2]Greene, Lawrence, *Kids Who Underachieve: Strategies for Understanding and Parenting the Academically Troubled Child*, Simon and Schuster, New York, 1986.

of them. Directly behind the chairs is a fire with animals and people walking in front of it. The images projected onto the cave wall from the fire appear to look like monsters. The people are unable to turn around and look at the simple reality, so to them based on their limited information, they see monsters.

PLATO'S CAVE ANALOGY

Wade, one of my 9th graders, was a My Way or the Highway Underachiever. Although he was extremely bright and capable, he nor his parents thought it was necessary to do what it takes to go to college or trade school.

"All I need to do is barely pass, so don't expect me to do anything extra. C's and D's are just fine. Once I graduate, I'll work full-time at my dad's autobody shop, and someday, I'll own it."

"Don't you think advanced training in how to run a business, how to advertise your business, or formal mechanic training might help you become a better owner?"

"My dad didn't go to college, and he does just fine . . . so no. Why bother?"

I tried everything I could to get Wade to widen his vision, but it is impossible to teach kids from where we want them to be. Instead, we must stand inside their worldview and do what we can to encourage them to stretch their thinking and grow.

When Wade was a senior, I convinced him to take a nonrequired online business marketing class . . . but that's as far as I got with him. He ended up owning his father's shop, which he still successfully runs today. Obviously, higher education is not for everyone, but at the time I felt like I was selling Wade short if I didn't at least try to untap his potential.

#2 Conformist Underachiever

This type of underachiever is more concerned with fitting in socially than doing well academically.

Miranda, a highly intelligent 5th grader, was referred to me by her teacher.

"I watched Miranda erase four correct answers on her social studies test, and intentionally change them to wrong answers before she turned it in. This brought her down from an A to a B. When I asked her why she did it, she denied the whole thing. Why would she choose to underperform on purpose? I am at a loss."

I pulled Miranda from class the next day.

"Your teacher tells me you messed up your social studies test score on purpose. Is that true?"

"Kinda," Miranda answered.

Why would you want to do that?"

"I don't want to be on the nerd wall!"

"What?"

"Everyone who gets 100% on a test gets their name up on the WALL of AMAZING!"

The last time, I was the only one who made it, and everyone called me a nerd. I'm never doing that again!"

I met with the teacher again and encouraged her to change the criteria for the WALL of AMAZING and use it to spotlight improvements vs perfection. After a few weeks, most of her students had their names up on the wall, and it became COOL to improve. It didn't take long for Miranda to do what it took to be up on the wall again.

#3 Distracted Learner Underachiever

This underachiever, despite being very intelligent, may not have the focus to sit still long enough and listen to instructions. Executive function deficits may also inhibit abilities to successfully complete assignments and tasks.

I grew up in the '60s and '70s, before teachers were aware of ADHD. Back then, they called it "BRAT" and I had it . . . BAD! I remember my dad telling me, "Juli, you are the only person I know who can be in seven rooms at once!" I seriously thought my name was "No Juli!" To me, having ADHD is like trying to watch a three-ring circus while attempting to learn a foreign language. There is always so much going on in my head, and keeping all my plates spinning in the right direction is a true art form.

One day, when I was in first grade, my teacher tied me to my chair with dental floss. Not to punish me, but to gently remind me to keep from getting out of my seat. Her goal was to keep me on task and prevent me from distracting others during seat work time. Her strategy didn't work very well. I just moved from place to place in the classroom with my chair stuck to my backside, and other kids laughed at me." This was my first memory of feeling humiliated.

The next day, I was bound and determined NOT to get tied to the chair ever again. I remember sitting in my seat, trying to keep my feet on the floor, butt in the chair, and hands to myself. I didn't hear one word my teacher said that day, because it took everything I had to simply stay seated.

We have come a long way since then, and looking back, I am not angry with that teacher. She was only trying to help me. Ironically, she ended up teaching me what NOT to do when you have a student who is a VERB! (Note: a "VERB" is a kid who is always doing something – only sometimes, it's the wrong something.)

#4 Rebel/Defiant Underachiever

This type of underachiever may question authority. They often use defiance and disruptive behavior as a defense to avoid facing their own fear of failure. TJ, the student in chapter one who filled my backpack full of rocks, is an example of a Rebel/Defiant Underachiever.

#5 Class Clown Underachiever

This type of underachiever thrives on attention, both negative and positive, and will go to great lengths to steal every molecule of oxygen in the room. They may also feel the need to use clowning to draw attention away from things they are struggling with such as anxiety, bullying, low self-esteem, trouble with social skills, or learning difficulties.

Sammy was an adorable 4th grade boy. Everyone loved him, and he knew it! Sammy's mom worked three jobs, and he and his two younger siblings spent an incredible amount of time at home with their father. Sammy craved attention, especially from adult females. He had his teacher wrapped around his little finger.

"Sammy is full-time job! He makes my classroom interesting, and some-times interesting has its challenges," she would often say. I'm not sure how she did it, but Sammy's teacher figured out a way to motivate him to work harder than any of his other teachers had in the past. She knew how to effectively pick her battles with this kid. Sammy had the ability to gain peer support for every stunt he attempted. He was a master at avoiding his schoolwork and pulling everyone else off task, including his teachers.

One day, I walked into Sammy's classroom to drop off a form. He was crawl-ing under desks, pretending to be the classroom puppy. Everyone was petting him. The teacher was busy working one on one with another student - who hap-pened to be the only kid on task. "Pet puppy Sammy quickly, and then keep work-ing on your activity sheets," I heard his teacher say. Just as I was leaving, I overheard a student whispering to Sammy, "Hey come over here and eat my paper. Then

I can say, "Hey look! My dog ate my homework!" Of course, Sammy immediately did it and tore the paper to shreds with his teeth. I'm not sure what happened after that . . . not sure I want to know either!

#6 Bricks But No Foundation Underachiever

This is the kid that has everything they need to achieve, but environmental circumstances that are out of their control prohibit them from reaching their true potential. To me, this can be the most heartbreaking type of underachiever, because all the materials needed to build the house are present, but the foundation is cracking and falling apart. Consider Maslow's triangle: It is impossible to self-actualize if your basic needs in life become compromised.

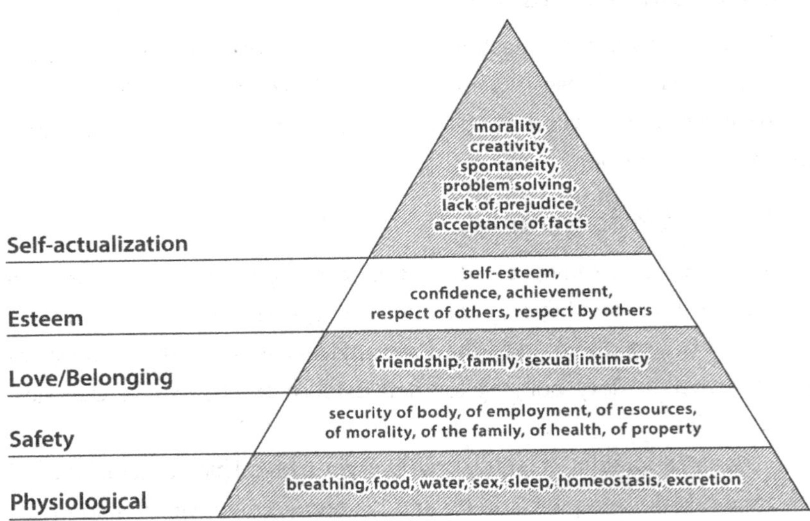

When Jill was in 10th grade, she was an AP honor roll student at the top of her class. She was also a three-sport varsity athlete, involved in student council, and an active member of the debate team. Her goal was to become a business law attorney. Tragically, in October of her junior year, Jill's mother was killed in a car accident. Jill was the oldest of seven kids, and her father worked two full-time jobs to keep the family financially afloat. After the accident, Jill became instant "fill-in mom." She transferred out of her AP classes, withdrew from all extracurricular activities, and shortened her school day to mornings only. At the semester break, Jill dropped out of school completely, and to my knowledge never returned.

Reversing Underachievement

To reverse underachievement and prevent underperformance, it is crucial to figure out what we are doing wrong, and how we can do things differently to improve.

There are many factors that contribute to underachieving. A partial list of these factors is printed below. Students, families, schools, and society are all collectively responsible.

Student Causes of Underachievement:

- Social Immaturity
- No Future Goals
- Behavior Problems
- Lack of Motivation
- Negative Peer Pressure
- Low Self-Worth
- Low Confidence Level
- Fear of Failure
- Academic Holes
- Lack of Executive Function Skills (study skills, organization, time management, etc.)

Parent/Family Causes of Underachievement:

- Instability
- Inability to Be in Charge (Easily Manipulated)
- Considering Education as a Low Priority
- Putting Too Much Pressure on a Child
- Inability to Guide Child Toward Responsibility and Independence
- Not Wanting Children to Experience Discomfort

School (Teachers, Mental Health Professionals, Administration) Causes of Underachievement:

- Lack of a Variety of Teaching Styles
- Impossible Standards
- Low Expectations
- Lack of Patience
- Reactive vs Proactive
- Being Too Helpful (Thinking for Your Students)
- Being Too Strict, Repressive, and Inflexible
- Expecting Students to Conform to Your Style as Opposed to Adapting to Theirs

Society Causes of Underachievement:

- Low Level of Respect for Teachers/Education
- Lack of Empathetic Understanding of the Challenges Teachers Are Facing
- Buy Now Pay Later Attitude

- Glorifying Instant Wealth and Glamour (Professional Sports, Music Industry, Professional Video Gamers)
- School Achievement Is Not Highly Valued
- Instant Gratification Mentality
- Online Influencer Effects

Reversing and preventing underachieving is also a collective effort. Students, families, schools, and society can all play a part.

What Students Can Do

There are many different things students can do individually to improve their achievement and untap their learning potential. Working to increase academic basic skills will help learning become more fluid and less stressful. Setting appropriate long- and short-term goals and celebrating the meeting of those goals will make going to school feel more purposeful and increase self-confidence. Discovering areas of high interest outside of school and improving independent learning strategies can increase motivation and effort. Developing better study skills and becoming more organized (brain, body stuff) can save time and improve overall performance. Hanging out with positive influencing peers can enhance better decision-making. And finally, if kids will make themselves a part of the system, and authentically learn to understand its flaws, they can use their talents to change it from within as opposed to ineffectively fighting it from the outside.

What Parents/Families Can Do

Parents and families can do many things to increase student achievement. Most importantly, parents need to develop a positive parental attitude – be your child's parent, not their peer. Support your child's interests both in and outside school. Create realistic, enforceable, consistent consequences for misbehaviors. Value your child's education and let them know you do. Develop unconditional, positive regard for your child. You may not like or agree with the choices they make, but you love them, regardless of what they do. Encourage responsibility and independence. Recognize and celebrate your child's strengths and teach them to use those strengths to overcome their weaknesses. And always keep in mind that growing is rarely comfortable. Being uncomfortable is great motivation for change and growth.

What Teachers, Mental Health Professionals, and Administrators Can Do

As an educator, you can have a huge impact on boosting achievement – you just need to work hard in the most effective direction possible. To do that you must first value what you do. Teach because it's a choice, not an obligation. If you truly do not love teaching kids, find a different profession. We can't expect our students to buy in to learning if we are not authentically invested in teaching, and kids are maestros at spotting a fake.

Get to know each student. Every kid is an individual worthy of the time it takes to understand them. Never forget, without your students, you wouldn't have a job.

Teach yourself to recognize different student modalities and multiple intelligences. Everyone has unique strengths and weaknesses. Kids are and always will be more important than any content you are trying to teach them.

Keep in mind that every misbehavior you experience with a student results from an unmet need. Focus on discovering the "why" behind the "what." Dealing with the misbehavior puts a Band-Aid on the problem. Filling the unmet need eliminates it.

Always remember, teaching is an art, not a science. Do your best to match your teaching style to the needs of your kids. Every class is unique, needing a style all its own. Teaching styles, just like our kids, are like moldable clay that will continually change shape over time. Don't ever let yourself dry out and get crumbly. You are a talented artist with unlimited media sources that are just waiting for you to get creative!

Measure progress from where your students start from as opposed to where you expect them to end up. Find multiple creative ways to document learning as opposed to measuring it only on test grades and performance.

Create real-life problem-solving opportunities with actual solutions, that relate your content to the real world, making learning more applicable and meaningful.

Focus and build upon what your students "CAN DO," not what they "CAN'T DO!"

Demonstrate unconditional positive regard. Separate what a child does from who they are, and always offer up a clean slate.

Know what you teach so you can teach what you know. (If you are a Spanish teacher, you should not be expected to teach German!)

And most important of all, find a way to become genuinely significant in the lives of your students. We all want to feel like we matter. If you truly matter to your kids, they will do back flips to stay in your class. If you do not, they will do back flips to leave.

What Society Can Do

Society has the potential to make a big difference when it comes to achievement, but to do that, we need to fix our flawed system. We need to start competitively recruiting top candidates for education. Teaching must be authentically promoted by absolutely everyone as a desired and respected profession, not a second career choice.

I have done numerous school presentations in Asia, where they treat their teachers like gold. The respect that kids, parents, and community show toward educators and schools is immeasurable. There is genuine truth in the quote, "If you want to feel worthy, respected, honored, and appreciated as a teacher, teach in Asia!"

We need to develop a campaign for appreciating all aspects of our educational system and effectively increase the pay of educators. Our kids are our future! They are what really matters! Educators have one of the most significant and important jobs, yet current salaries in no way reflect our purpose. How can we possibly recruit the best of the best to teach our children if we are not willing to pay people what they are worth? To increase educational funding, we need to first make it appealing for corporate America to become more involved. Increasing tax donation incentives, establishing person-to-person relationships, and developing more effective internship/recruiting programs could make a huge impact toward repairing our system.

Conclusion

Underachievement is a multifaceted problem. To reverse it appears overwhelming, but if we look at it as a continuum, we can all work together to effectively reduce it. To visualize this problem, look at the car below as a typical underachieving student.

If the student, the family, the educators, and society make just one change, underachievement starts to reverse itself.

With two changes from all fronts, the effect is even greater.

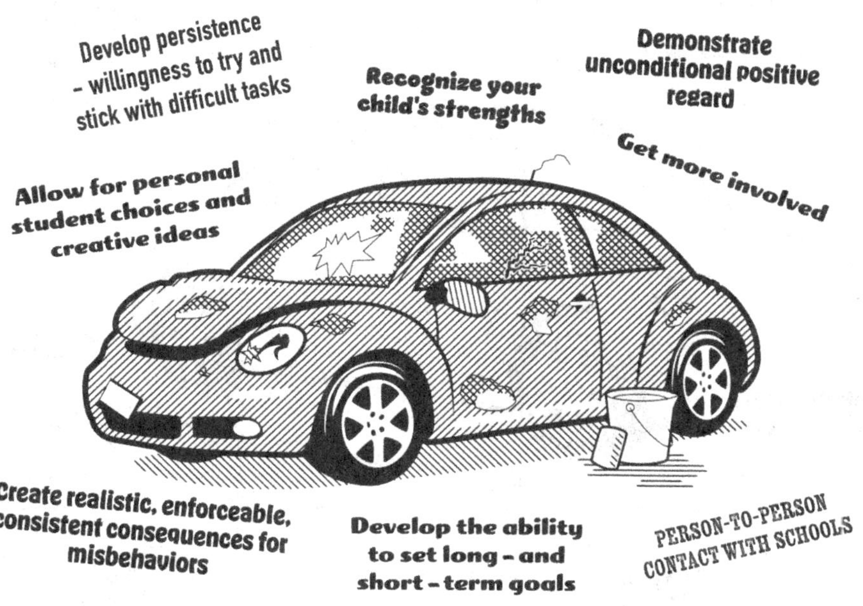

Three changes. . .

More changes . . .

If we lived in a perfect world and all changes were made, underachieving would become extinct.

Every change we choose to make when it comes to reversing underachievement helps!

Worth Remembering

- Underachieving students have a significant gap between their ability and what they achieve in school. Performance does not reflect potential.
- There are six types of underachievers:

  My Way or the Highway Underachiever – This type of underachiever may be stifled from seeing the situation from another point of view. They tend to do just enough to get by and rarely perform to their potential. They do not see the benefit of exerting more effort.

  Conformist Underachiever – This type of underachiever is more concerned with fitting in socially than doing well academically.

  Distracted Learner Underachiever – This underachiever, despite being very intelligent, may not have the focus to sit still long enough and listen to instructions. Executive function deficits may also inhibit abilities to successfully complete assignments and tasks.

  Rebel/Defiant Underachiever – This type of underachiever may question authority. They often use defiance and disruptive behavior as a defense to avoid facing their own fear of failure.

  Class Clown Underachiever – This type of underachiever thrives on attention, both negative and positive, and will go to great lengths to steal every molecule of oxygen in the room. They may also feel the need to use clowning to draw attention away from things they are struggling with such as anxiety, bullying, low self-esteem, trouble with social skills, or learning difficulties.

  Bricks But No Foundation Underachiever – This is the kid that has everything they need to achieve, but environmental circumstances that are out of their control prohibit them from reaching their true potential.

- Underachievement is collectively caused by the actions of students, parents/families, educators, and society.
- To reverse underachievement, everyone must do things differently. Even the slightest change can have a big impact.

Worth Trying

- Value what you do!
- Get to know each student.

- Recognize different modalities and multiple intelligences.
- Focus on filling the need that is causing the misbehavior.
- Do your best to match your teaching style to the needs of your kids.
- Measure progress from where your students start from as opposed to where you expect them to end up.
- Create real-life problem-solving opportunities with actual solutions, that relate your content to the real world, making learning more applicable and meaningful.
- Focus and build upon what your students "CAN DO," not what they "CAN'T DO!"
- Demonstrate unconditional positive regard. Separate what a child does from who they are and always offer up a clean slate.
- Become significant to your students.
- Have Students Complete the What Are Your Gifts? Activity below:

08 Teaching Kids the Importance of GRIT!

"**GRIT – G**enerating **R**elentless **I**nner **T**oughness!"

–Tamara Zentic

In her book, *Grit & Bear It*, Tamara Zentic uses the quote above, saying GRIT is the act of generating relentless inner toughness.[1] Angela Duckworth puts it slightly another way, "Grit is having passion and perseverance to achieve long-term goals."[2]

Either way, *GRIT* gives us a mental toughness to stick with things and keep going, even in the face of adversity. To have GRIT, effort must become secondary to purpose.

Having GRIT is a true asset that will serve our kids for life. It is a powerful predictor of success in all aspects including academics, personal goal setting, career achievement, and athletic achievement. GRIT can be strengthened and developed over time. It may take extra effort, creativity, and time to help our students build GRIT, but the payoff will serve them for decades!

GRIT is something that is not innate. It needs to be learned. However, we all start to develop the foundation of being gritty at a very early age.

When a baby is starting to walk, every core principle of GRIT is activated. Babies don't quit trying if they fall over. Instead, they *persevere*, get back up, and demonstrate a willingness to try again.

Babies are curious and are highly motivated to explore their environment. This *motivation* increases their effort, even when they experience a setback.

(*Continued*)

---

[1]Zentic, Tamara, *Grit & Bear It*, Boys Town Press, Omaha, 2014.
[2]Duckworth, Angela, *Grit: The Power of Passion and Perseverance*, Scribner, New York, 2016, p. 2.

Babies don't just take off walking. Instead, they naturally *practice* and develop "baby steps" (pulling themselves up, walking around furniture, etc.) that lead toward their goal.

When you were learning to walk, you stumbled, fell, and tipped over. Even though it was very uncomfortable at times, you kept trying. You *overcame failure and learned from your mistakes*.

Look at you now! You are an expert at walking, and you have your GRIT to thank!

The Power of GRIT

Manteo Mitchell used the power of GRIT to accomplish the unthinkable:

> "During the 2012 Olympics, Manteo Mitchell was running the first leg of the qualifying round for the 4 × 400 relay. With half of a lap to go, Mitchell stepped down on the turf and felt a pop in his calf.
>
> 'As soon as I took the first step past the 200-meter mark, I felt it break. I heard it. I even put out a little war cry, but the crowd was so loud you couldn't hear it. I wanted to just lie down. It felt like somebody literally snapped my leg in half. I had a choice . . . keep running or lose the race. To me, it was never much of a choice.'
>
> Immediately after struggling to complete the hand off to teammate Josh Mance, Manteo awkwardly hobbled to the side of the track. Mance, Tony McQuay, and Bryshon Nellum rallied to get the US to the finish line in 2 minutes 58.87 seconds, posting the fastest ever first round of the relay at the Olympics. Later that afternoon, Manteo Mitchell found out that he had broken his fibula."[3]

How can we teach young people to mirror the GRIT exhibited by extraordinary people?

Considering the many unique challenges we face daily in the world of education, having GRIT can be an invaluable asset to both educators and students. GRIT is the key ingredient for success in every aspect of life. But teaching today's kids to be gritty is a lot harder than it used to be.

---

[3]Elliot, Helene, "U.S. Relay Runner Manteo Mitchell Finished Race on Broken Leg," *Los Angeles Times*, August 9, 2012, https://www.latimes.com/sports/olympics/la-xpm-2012-aug-09-la-sp-on-manteo-mitchell-20120809-story.html.

So often, when our students are faced with challenges that require extra effort, they tend to shut down or switch directions. In the past decade, I've heard so many people say, "Today's kids are soft. They are either afraid to try because they think they might fail, or they become frustrated very easily and quit."

We need to look beyond the behaviors of avoidance and giving up easily and consider the reasons behind these behaviors. Kids quit too easily because confronting and overcoming struggle requires uncomfortable effort. Uncomfortable effort used to be a much bigger part of daily life. Now, thanks to technology, we do everything we can to eliminate experiencing uncomfortable effort:

- We no longer carry our luggage; now we pull it on wheels, and some suitcases are even motorized!
- We push a button to get instant information vs making the effort to drive to a library to research information.
- We push a button to score a point vs mentally and physically practicing and/or playing a sport and scoring a point in a live game.
- We push a button and have exactly what we want delivered to our doorstep vs taking the time to shop at numerous stores looking for what we want and need.
- We push a button to get a reaction and/or feedback from thousands vs talking to others in person and receiving real-time face-to-face reactions.
- We now can often work from home in our own controlled environment vs physically preparing ourselves and traveling to a workplace environment that is much less in our control.

How can we expect our students to embrace and endure struggle when the society we live in seems to be doing everything it can to eliminate uncomfortable effort? Our kids are not getting softer, but their struggle muscles are getting weaker due to lack of use. Life is full of challenging encounters, and school is practice for life. So, if we truly want our kids to succeed beyond the classroom, we need to teach them how to get more gritty.

Don't think of building GRIT as "one more thing we now have to teach our kids." Instead, think of it as something you sprinkle into what you are already doing every day. If getting a great education was like making a pot of soup, GRIT would be the seasoning you add in along the way to make the soup savory. The meat and the vegetables each with their own unique flavor are the subjects we teach our students. The broth, like our daily classroom life, allows the flavors to interact and combine, and the seasoning, GRIT, makes the soup taste so good that its worth eating and even making another batch.

How to Teach GRIT

Everyone has the capacity to develop GRIT. It may be easier for some than others, but GRIT can be learned and cultivated over time through effort, practice, reward, and celebration. To build GRIT, kids must set goals that they genuinely want to achieve, be willing and feel safe enough to exercise their struggle muscles over time, and like Manteo Mitchell, make the amount of uncomfortable effort they put forth secondary to achieving their overall goals. That's a lot easier said than done! However, if a child can visualize the importance and personal benefits of achieving their goal, and/or discover ways to enjoy the working experience needed to meet that goal, getting "more gritty" is doable. Without vision of benefits, desire, and joy, uncomfortable effort becomes too uncomfortable, and GRIT becomes inert.

The following GRIT acronym is a great tool to keep in mind.

G – Growth Mindset
R – Reason
I – Inspiration
T – Talk

Here's how it works.

G – Growth Mindset

The tagline for my book, *Bubble Gum Brain*, is "Ready, Get Mindset . . . GROW!" and it shows kids (as well as adults) that becoming is better than being, which can open the door to a whole new world of possibilities. But how?

- **Great people make great mistakes!** Help kids understand that making mistakes is both necessary and okay. When kids can begin to feel safe about making mistakes, they become free to figure out what does and does not work. They also develop more courage to explore new challenges.
- **Avoid blaming.** When we blame others for our mistakes, we lose an opportunity to learn. Instead, teach kids to own and talk about their mistakes. It's much more important to strive for growth through learning than it is to be perfect.
- **Ask B-R-A-I-N S-T-R-E-T-C-H-I-N-G questions** that lead kids to look at situations from different perspectives. When we tell someone how to solve a problem, we inhibit them from thinking strategically. Instead, encourage kids to think outside, inside, around, below, and above the challenge by asking thought-provoking questions which build confidence and internal feelings of capability.
- **Teach kids the POWER of YET!** To learn, we need to struggle. Struggle is a good thing. It means our brains are growing and building new pathways, and that rarely feels comfortable. Instead of saying "I can't do it" . . . say "I can't do it YET!"

- **Encourage and model the practice of not giving up.** Keep in mind that the process of struggle often becomes more valuable than finding a solution to a problem. Persistence is key.
- **Applaud uncomfortable effort and celebrate learning.** Effort is the vehicle to learning and improving.

R – Reason

What is your reason? Why is doing this thing important to you? Having a reason for action can significantly influence building GRIT. A strong reason or purpose can ignite passion, boost motivation, foster engagement, and build enthusiasm. Reason makes uncomfortable effort seem worth it. The struggle needs to pay off or it isn't worth the effort.

Remember the two questions most every student asks:

"Why should I do this?"
"When I do it, what do I get?"

"It's difficult for a flower to crave water if it is not thirsty."

I – Inspiration

Who inspires you and can help you succeed? GRIT is highly impacted and cultivated thru inspiration. Inspiration from watching and learning from an authentic role model can provide pathways for a plan of action, a sense of relatable struggle, and proof that uncomfortable struggle will and can pay off. Even more important, observing and listening to someone who has used their GRIT to achieve a similar goal builds hope, encouragement, motivation, and validation.

As a high school student, not much seemed to inspire me academically. I did what I needed to do to get good grades so my parents wouldn't freak out on me, and I did everything I could to avoid going to class – including pretending to be sick and writing bogus "Please excuse Julia from class today" notes from my parents. I basically took much of my life at school for granted.

I sat by Veronica in honors English my sophomore year. She wore coke bottle-lens glasses but had a really pretty face when she took them off to clean them. Veronica used a wheelchair due to cerebral palsy and had very little control over her legs and one of her arms. We weren't exactly friends, but she was always really nice to me and I enjoyed talking to her.

One day, our teacher gave us a "compare and contrast" writing assignment and paired us up to discuss what we were going to write about. I got partnered with Veronica, only she wasn't in class that day. I sat there alone, full of dread thinking, "I hate to write!" "This assignment is so bogus!" "What a stupid topic!" etc.

Ten minutes before the bell rang, in came Veronica.

"Where have you been?" I asked.

"I couldn't get up today. I was too sore and I woke up with a migraine so I had to stay in bed 'til 7 am."

"You got up at 7 and you're still late? It's 10:30!"

"Well, I usually have to get up at 5 am so I can stretch out my legs and back. Then, I have to do a muscle stimulation thing to get the muscles in my back to relax so I can sit in my wheelchair. If I don't, it hurts too bad to sit. And, if I get a fever, which I do a lot, my mom won't let me come at all, so when I feel sick, I fake it and tell her I'm okay."

"You mean to tell me you have to get up at 5 am every day just so you can make it to school by 8 am?"

"Yes. I love coming to school. I'll do anything to get here."

Out of thin air, my "compare and contrast" story fell into my lap. I pretended to be sick and did everything I could think of to get out of going to school, while Veronica endured daily uncomfortable effort and pretended to be well so she could go to school. We both worked strategically, creatively, and very hard to accomplish opposing results. I talked to Veronica at length, and the more I heard, the more inspired and appreciative of her efforts I became.

I wrote the essay, turned it in, became great friends with Veronica, and that was that . . . until my junior year when my teacher asked if she could enter the essay into a national writing contest put on by the John F. Kennedy foundation that spotlighted an appreciation for people with disabilities.

Three months later, I was told that my essay had won. I was blown away. But this wasn't my award, it was Veronica's. She's the one who inspired me to write the essay. She's the one who showed me the power of GRIT. She's the one who made me appreciate being healthy enough to go to school.

And because of Veronica, I saw myself as an effective writer for the first time.

T – Talk

Talk! Talk! Talk! – "You have to say it if you want to do it!"

Talk about your goal and how you plan to meet it. Verbalizing your goals and plans through conversations with like-minded people can make them seem more real and achievable. It can increase your accountability, foster self-awareness, and develop your confidence. Also, discussing past successes can build hope for current challenges and fuel future success.

The Overall Environment

In her book *The Smartest Kids in the World*, Amanda Ripley compares the high-achieving education systems of Poland, Finland, and South Korea with the struggling education system of the United States.[4] She attributes school success in these three countries to creating an overall environment for kids both at home and at school that expects a strong, rigorous work ethic and provides wraparound support from both teachers and parents. Ripley's research unveils many factors that foster school achievement including:

- To buy into school, kids must be reminded of its purpose every day and all day. They also must see the value in that purpose.
- Daily Joyful Rigor – Success in education stems from having a focus on effort and persistence. Effort drastically increases when kids are enjoying what they are doing. Joyful Rigor is active, physically engaging learning through doing, as opposed to passive listening and watching.
- World-class educators authentically LOVE teaching, have a vision for where they are going, and possess the tools they need to determine if they have lost their way.

---

[4]Ripley, Amanda, *The Smartest Kids in the World*, Simon & Schuster Paperbacks, New York, 2013.

- World-class educators embrace a culture of perpetual change to keep growing and improving.
- World-class educators set and enforce predictable boundaries (physical, psychological, and emotional).
- World-class educators collaborate effectively with colleagues and receive support from leaders and administrators.
- World-class educators authentically model persistence, integrity, self-control, and a genuine desire to make a positive difference.

One of my favorite elementary principals is Mrs. Jones, and she shared a powerful kid GRIT story with me:

> I spell GRIT K-Y-L-A-R. Kylar was just starting 3rd grade when I met him. It was my first year as principal at a new school when he landed in my office for throwing a ball at another kid's face on the playground. He wasn't at all how I pictured him.
>
> I'd already heard a lot about Kylar from my staff. I was told by numerous teachers and paras that he had a very difficult time telling the truth, was a gifted manipulator, had a short fuse, and was highly competitive. I got the impression that this kid had dug himself a very deep hole at school in just three short years and figured he might meet my "frequent flyer" protocol.
>
> There he sat, looking at me with bright brown eyes, blonde hair, and freckles that looked like they were drawn on with a fine point marker.
>
> "Tell me your story, Kylar. What happened?"
>
> "Johnathan said the ball hit me and it didn't, so I threw it at him because he said I lied."
>
> "Did the ball hit you?"
>
> "No . . . well . . . it hit my shirt, but it didn't hit me."
>
> A few minutes later, Kylar's parents arrived at the school and joined us in our meeting. Apparently, there was an ongoing plan in place. . . . Every time he ended up with an office referral, his parents were called and asked to immediately come to the school.
>
> Kylar's mom started in on him as she walked through the door.
>
> "What did you do this time? Do we need to make that call to military school? It's day one Kylar! You can't even be good for one day?"
>
> Kylar crumbled into the back of his chair. He looked like a wilted balloon. I did everything I could to process through the incident quickly and reassure his parents that we could work through this at school so they wouldn't need to give him more consequences at

home. Kylar read into that immediately, started to reinflate, and shot me a sincere, hopeful glance.

After our discussion ended, we all left my office and walked into the hallway toward the front door. A few minutes later, I heard Kylar's mom tell him, "Hey, go say hi to Ricky. Isn't he one of your friends?"

"I don't like him mom; he's a bully. He's mean to kids."

Interesting . . . I thought to myself. A bully who was also a target?

That afternoon, I met with Kylar to figure out his needs and come up with a plan.

"What's missing at school for you, Kylar? What do you want that you don't have?"

"I want to have friends to play with. Nobody likes me at this school."

"Well, that's a great answer. But to have friends, you need to figure out how to be a better friend. I can teach you how to do it, but it's going to take a lot of hard work and a lot of time."

"I want to work hard. I want to do better."

I realized right away this kid didn't see himself as a bully. He was an only child who was doing everything he could to be liked, validated, and accepted by his peers. In addition, Kylar was genuinely trying to find a way to survive fear with the skill set that he had.

"My dad told me that if I didn't stop getting in trouble, he'd send me away to military school and make me live there with people I don't know. I try to be good, but sometimes, I mess up. Then I lie so I don't get in trouble. I don't want my parents to get rid of me. I don't like it when I get angry and I don't want to be mean. I want to do better."

I knew I couldn't help Kylar if he was under a threat cloud, so I made a deal with him that I would do everything I could to make what happens at school stay at school. We created a contract to meet and talk on Monday mornings, and I set him up with a daily check-in and check-out plan. Now that I could see his reasoning behind his behavior, my goal was to help Kylar develop more effective communication skills and rebuild trust with both his peers and his teachers.

I met with Kylar's parents early in the process and informed them of our plan. They were extremely supportive, caring, competitive, hard-working people who only wanted the best for their son.

They were also very grateful that they didn't have to keep coming to school every time Kylar had an incident.

"When I was a boy, my dad threatened me with military school and it worked, so we tried it on Kylar as a last resort," his dad told me.

Obviously, they too were doing the very best that they could with the cards they had been dealt.

Restoring trust is not easy. It takes a lot of time, skill building, and hard work, but by midyear, things were starting to slightly improve. I was lucky enough to become Kylar's "person" at school. He learned quickly that even if I didn't like some of his choices, I genuinely cared about him. I'm pretty sure that made him try even harder because he didn't want to let me down.

We followed our plan throughout the year and continued to meet as needed through 4th grade. I remember being so impressed with this kid's ability to recognize his mistakes and his willingness to keep trying to improve. He worked on telling the truth, quick strategy building, empathy, how to apologize to others, and how to forgive others when they make mistakes.

Kylar's relationships with his teachers and his peers improved drastically, and his office referrals became few and far between. However, one day, in the middle of his 4th grade year, Kylar got into an uncharacteristic shoving match on the playground and once again ended up in my office.

"Oh no, what happened?"

"Rayne said I lied, and I didn't. I got mad at him and I pushed him down."

"What happened after that?"

"He shoved me hard and I fell. I was so angry inside, but I understood why he did it so I got up, took a really deep breath, looked at him and just walked away."

After processing through the event and accepting the consequences, I could tell that Kylar was still upset the following day.

"Are you angry at Rayne?" I asked.

"No, I'm really mad at myself for getting in trouble. I shouldn't have lost my temper. That was so dumb! I know better."

"Well, do you think you'll ever be able to forgive yourself?"

"Yeah maybe, because of the pillow."

"What pillow?"

"That pillow on the shelf in my classroom that says, MISTAKES ARE PROOF THAT YOU ARE TRYING. I am trying. I try hard every day. I shouldn't have pushed him in the first place. That was a big mistake. But I'm also a little bit proud of myself for walking away."

By the time Kylar was 10, he had tons of friends and was adored by his teachers. He had grown into a much more likable kid that most everyone trusted. At the end of 5th grade graduation, he gave me a big hug and whispered, "Thank you for helping me not quit on myself."

Looking back, I realize now how important having friends and feeling included must have been to Kylar. It took him three years, a few new skills, many failures, and a ton of practice to figure it all out. But Kylar is a great example of GRIT paying off. He never gave up on his goal even when others appeared to give up on him. Every time Kylar stumbled and fell, he struggled and got back up, because that's what he needed to do to get what he truly wanted.

Video Games Can Stifle GRIT

Recent studies indicate that over 90% of kids today play video games.[5]

Depending on the type of reward offered, video gaming can have bipolar impacts on the development and cultivation of GRIT. Video games that offer rewards for productive struggle can increase student engagement, teach kids to visualize growth and progress, and encourage them to learn from making mistakes. They also can teach kids to "follow the rules, acquire and practice skills, and apply those skills to achieve specific goals."[6]

However, games that focus on rewarding the product vs the process can unfortunately stifle GRIT. When winning accompanied by a dopamine release becomes relatively easy to attain, it conditions the brain to believe that success should not require a lot of effort. Quick wins, level-ups, and achievements that provide frequent and immediate rewards can potentially make it more difficult for kids to find motivation for real-life goals that require sustained effort, delayed gratification and harder work needed for long-term success.

On the flip side, video games that are extremely challenging may cause players to develop feelings of overall hopelessness. Continuous attempts resulting in

[5]Lager, Kyndle S., and German Corso. "Game Faces: How Digital Play Affects the Psychological Landscape of Youth," National Institute of Health, January 15, 2025, https://pmc.ncbi.nlm.nih.gov/articles/PMC11 828491/.
[6]Loo, Kara, "How Video Games Can Instill the Values Your Children Need for Success," Huffpost, September 19, 2014, https://www.huffpost.com/entry/how-video-games-can-insti_b_5852030.

a loss may convince a child's brain that effort is ineffective: "No matter how hard I try I can't win, so why even try?" Unfortunately, this learned helplessness result often transfers into other areas of life.

When it comes to building GRIT and video gaming, the overall key is balance. Excessive gaming and/or playing games that are too easy or too difficult can lead to decreased interpersonal skill development and disengagement from real-life challenges. Responsible gaming, on the other hand, can build resilience, foster hard work, and allow kids an opportunity to apply learned skills to real-life situations.

Worth Remembering

- GRIT is having passion and perseverance to achieve long-term goals.
- To have GRIT, effort must become secondary to purpose.
- GRIT is something that is not innate. It needs to be learned. However, we all start to develop the foundation of being gritty at a very early age.
- GRIT is the key ingredient for success in every aspect of life.
- Don't think of building GRIT as "one more thing we now have to teach our kids." Instead, think of it as something you sprinkle into what you are already doing every day.
- If a child can visualize the importance and personal benefits of achieving their goal, and/or discover ways to enjoy the working experience needed to meet that goal, cultivating GRIT becomes more doable.
- Without vision of benefits, desire, and joy, uncomfortable effort becomes too uncomfortable, and GRIT becomes inert.
- The GRIT acronym is a great tool to keep in mind: Growth mindset. Reason. Inspiration. Talk.
- Depending on the type of reward offered, video gaming can have bipolar impacts on the development and cultivation of GRIT.
- Video games that offer rewards for productive struggle can increase student engagement, teach kids to visualize growth and progress, and encourage them to learn from making mistakes.
- Games that focus on rewarding the product vs the process can unfortunately stifle GRIT because winning becomes too easy and dopamine release becomes too powerful.
- Games that are extremely challenging may cause players to develop feelings of overall hopelessness.

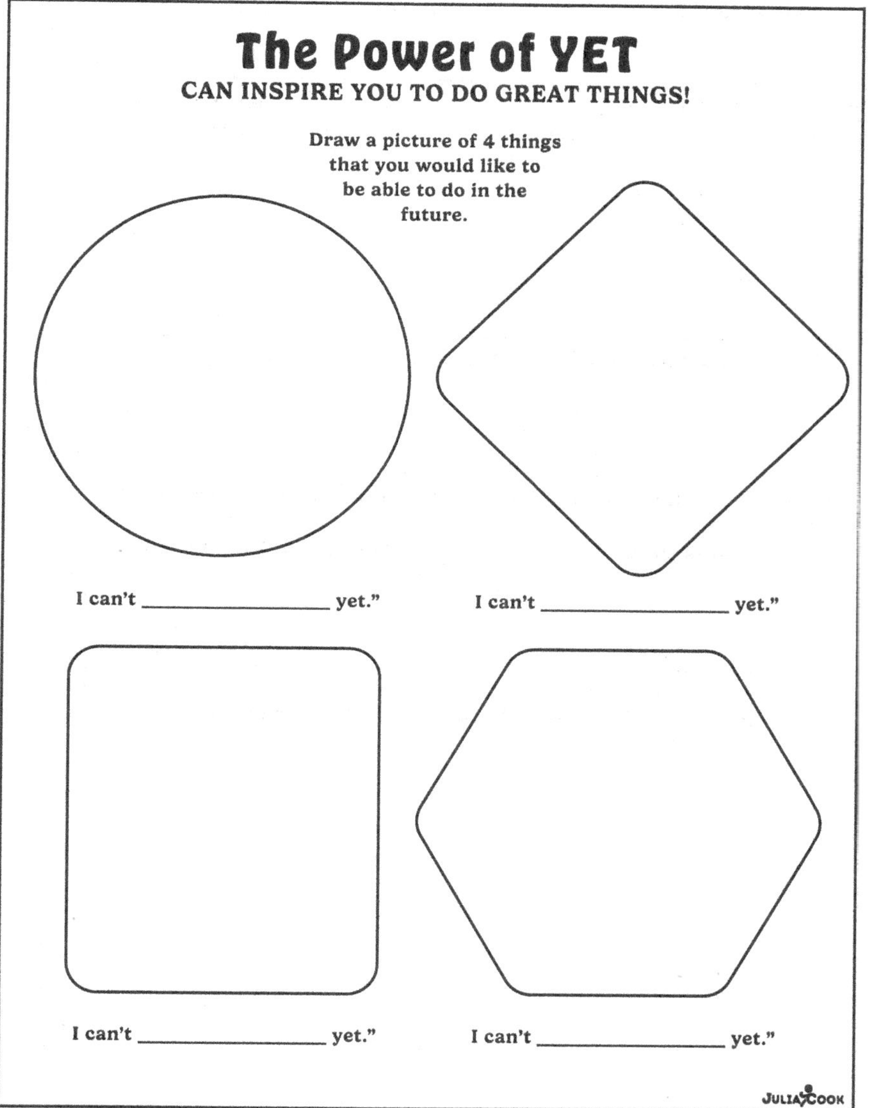
The Power of YET
CAN INSPIRE YOU TO DO GREAT THINGS!
Draw a picture of 4 things that you would like to be able to do in the future.
I can't _____________ yet."
I can't _____________ yet."
I can't _____________ yet."
I can't _____________ yet."
JULIA COOK

BUILDING GRIT!

I wish I could... (pick one thing off of your Power of Yet sheet)

____

List all of the resources you can use to help you meet your goal:	**What struggles have you encountered so far?**

How have your struggles helped you grow?

What small wins have you had and how did you celebrate them?

My wins so far: | **How I celebrated them:**

A picture of you when you make your wish come true:

JULIA COOK

What I Tell Parents

"Somewhere along the way, parents got the following message: To be a good parent I need to always be there to rescue my children when needed. This is far from the truth. A good parent allows their kids to struggle and sometimes even fail in a supportive environment. They provide their children with the tools and skills needed to migrate through life's tough situations and stand next to them in support."

–Mary Lynn Rodriquez

Kids don't come with instructions! That's one of the many reasons why being a parent is one of the hardest jobs on the planet. What might work well with one child, may not work with another. When you hear the words of your own parent coming out of your mouth and they don't work on your kid, parenting becomes even more difficult.

Parenting is an ever-evolving, "learn-by-doing" profession. You can never know it all, and you may feel like you never know enough. The trick to being a successful parent is to raise your child to become resilient and live successfully in a world where others may not love and care about them as much as you do.

The key to being a good parent is knowing how to build a healthy relationship with your child that will endure many lifelong phases and challenges.

As I said in an earlier chapter, there are two things all human relationships must have to survive: **trust** and **communication**. If one or both become fractured, the relationship will ultimately suffer.

You may go through times when you don't particularly like your child, and for sure times when they don't like you, but if your child can trust you and talk to you and vice versa, you will always be able to have a functional relationship.

Be Appropriately Honest

Kids are continually missing pieces from the "Making Sense Out of My World" puzzle.

They often ask us questions that are very difficult to answer because what we want to tell them may not end up being the truth, and if that happens, and our kids find out, trust is damaged.

I received this letter from a parent a few years ago.

Dear Julia Cook:

I hope this email finds you well. I had the opportunity to attend one of your parenting sessions at my daughter's school last month. You told us that if we ever have a question, we can contact you.

This morning as I pulled up to school, my little girl opened the door, looked up at me with her 6-year-old serious eyes and asked, "Mommy, will there be a shooter at my school today?"

Before I could catch my breath to answer, a little girl in her class called out her name and she quickly kissed me goodbye, stepped out of the car and shut the door. "Saved by a peer. . . . Whew!"

How am I supposed to answer a question like that? I know she will eventually ask me again, and the last thing I want is a child who is too afraid to go to school. Why do our kids have to grow up thinking about horrible things like this? Any advice is much appreciated.

Sincerely,
Annika Jones

Here was my answer:

Dear Annika,

Kids have a way of asking us the hardest questions!

I'm sure at the time, your heart was telling you to sooth your daughter's fears by saying, "Oh no, don't worry about that. It won't happen here." But sadly in today's world, school shootings can happen anywhere.

The next time a tough question is asked and you don't quite know what to do, take a breath and say, "Wow! That is a really great question. I don't even have the words right now to answer it, but I will figure out the right answer for you, and we will talk about this as soon as I do that."

You are a parent and you are not expected to know it all . . . EVER! But you are your child's expert! Never try to wing it when you are not sure how to answer a question. Instead, put your answer on hold, do a little research, and take some time to figure out the best words to use.

For this situation, I would try to find out why she might have asked such a difficult question. Is there something going on at school or in your community that might be causing your daughter to worry about a school shooter? Did she see something online or on TV? Then, if she asks you again say, "Nobody truly knows the answer to that question, but just know, everyone in our town is working really hard to keep you safe at school, and together . . . we are very STRONG!"

If she doesn't happen to ask you again, you may want to reassure her by saying something like, "If you ever have a question about anything, you know that I will always do my best to answer it, and I will always tell you the truth."

It's natural for kids to continually try make sense out of their world by filling in the missing gaps. To be a successful parent, you must build a strong relationship with your child based on trust and communication. If you tell her what you want her to hear and it ends up not being the truth, trust will fracture trust, and your relationship will suffer.

I hope this helps. Reach out again any time.

BEST!
Julia Cook

Always do your best to tell your children the truth when they ask questions. Make sure your answers are appropriate for their current worldview and information needs. So often, we give kids more information than they are looking for and end up confusing them and/or causing them anxiety. A great way to prevent yourself from doing this is to simply ask questions.

For example:

CHILD: "What's sex about anyway?"
PARENT: "Wow! That's a great question! What do you know about it? Tell me what you've heard, and I'll help you fill in the blanks."

Teach and Model Good Communication Skills

Thanks to the digital world, teaching kids to communicate effectively can be a challenge at times. Many young people are willing to text you their whole life story, yet they feel very insecure when talking to people face-to-face. Although it is imperative that our kids develop effective digital communication skills, *having strong face-to-face communication skills is equally if not more valued and important.*

Not long ago, if a customer was physically in a store shopping and the phone rang, the store clerk would ignore the call and continue to wait on the "real live person." A few weeks ago, while in the checkout line at a grocery store, the checker got a text, stopped scanning my groceries, pulled out his phone, read the text, responded, put his phone back in his pocket and then resumed checking. This happened three times while I stood there waiting to pay.

Although this may not be the norm (yet), it made me feel like I didn't matter much to that store, not to mention the fact that the checker didn't say two words to me the entire time. Trying not to judge and thinking about what I preach: every behavior is a result of an unmet need, I thought, "maybe this checker is nonverbal. Or maybe he is enduring a situation of personal crisis and is doing his best to survive." Without even an attempt at communication, how could I tell?

As I exited the store, I glanced back at the checker. He was laughing and joking around with another employee. Consequently, I won't be shopping at that store again. In my brain, the customer should matter. Without customers, stores go out of business!

If you teach your child how to feel comfortable communicating in face-to-face situations, relationship building will become much easier and less stressful. Good communication skills will also help your child feel seen, heard, and validated by others.

There are many ways to help your child build confidence when communicating with others face-to-face.

For example:

- Ask creative open-ended questions:

  "What did you do at school today?"
  "Nothing."

  Sound familiar? Next time, try this approach:

  "What was the best thing that happened to you today at school?"
  "What was the worst thing that happened to you today at school?"

  Then, talk about your best and worst parts of your day, and weave in a conversation.

- Model effective face-to-face communication for your child by making it a point to talk with others whenever possible as opposed to using text, email, or messaging.
- Model and emphasize the power and advantages of reading body language and expressions while having a conversation. Video chat can often become a safe bridge to in-person conversation.
- Unless the person on the other end of your phone call or email has a 911 emergency, make your child a priority over your device. If they ask a question or strike up a conversation while you are on your phone or computer, stop what you are doing and talk to them. The email, the text, and the post can wait. We cannot expect our kids to be respectful with technology if we are disrespectful to them while using it. Parenting while on your phone or tablet tells your child that screens are as important or even more important than they are.
- Have your child write thank you notes using actual pen and paper. Help them mail or deliver those notes in person. This extra effort will help your child see the benefits of taking time to communicate more effectively. It can also improve their written conversation skills, and lay a more thought-out groundwork for effective life conversation. They will also gain more appreciation and respect from others.
- Create everyday scenarios that actively involve your children in face-to-face communication:
  1. Let your child order their food at a restaurant.
  2. Have your child ask a store clerk where to find an item.
  3. Let your child interview an expert about a topic they find interesting as opposed to doing research online.
  4. Allow them to call and make an appointment to get their hair cut.

Building strong communication skills regardless of the situation takes practice. Because of the world we live in, your child will naturally get plenty of experience with digital communication. However, in-person communication practice opportunities are, and will continue to become, more and more difficult for your child to naturally experience. Making the effort to teach your children how to communicate with people effectively on all fronts will foster future relationship building strengths, and build self-advocating skills.

Know the Succeed Needs

Parents typically play the best hand they can with the cards they've been dealt to equip their children with everything they need to win in the world. But what exactly are those needs? What do we really need to teach our children so they can grow into self-sufficient, healthy, happy adults?

I was asked some years ago to write a children's book on careers. The philosophy behind this request was to help teachers creatively introduce career possibilities to kids at a young age through a storybook.

"How do we prepare our kids and teach them how to 'get there' if they have no idea where they want to go?"

Do you know how many careers there are??? I only had 30 pages to work with! Ugh!!!

After doing my research, I decided to gear my story around shoes because most everyone can relate to a cool pair of shoes. The main goal of the book was to figuratively have children "walk in a lot of soles" so they could determine a possible fit for a future career path, hence the title: *What Shoes Will You Wear?*[1]

While researching this topic, I discovered from a variety of sources there's a consistent list of qualities needed in life to become successful in the 21st century. The Big List varies somewhat year to year, depending on the research, but the philosophy behind it is regardless of what career path you take in life, the more of these skills and qualities you have, the more successful you will become.

I like to tell parents if I could give you a recipe for building successful kids, the following list would be the ingredients.

Because the list is long, I needed to make it palatable and fun, so I wove it into a rhyme.

"It's your choice to choose when you grow up
What you want to become.
But no matter what your choice ends up being,
There are <u>SKILLS</u> that you must learn."

---

[1] Cook, Julia, *What Shoes Will You Wear?* National Center for Youth Issues, Chattanooga, TN, 2014.

"You need to be able to **TALK** to people,
and you need to be able to **LISTEN**.
You've got to be able to **READ** and **WRITE**,
and **SCIENCE** and **MATH** can't be missing."
"It helps if you can **THINK CREATIVELY**
and **HAVE GOOD REASONING SKILLS**.
If you can **MAKE GOOD DECISIONS** and **PROBLEM SOLVE**,
then you'll be the REAL DEAL!"
"The most important skill you need
is to never let yourself stop **LEARNING**.
Situations, people, and environments change,
and knowledge determines your journey."
"No matter what you end up wearing
to work when you grow up,
there are _QUALITIES_ that you must have
each day when you show up."
"You need to be **RESPONSIBLE**,
and **GET TO WORK ON TIME**.
You need to have **SELF-CONFIDENCE**,
and having **INTEGRITY** can make you shine."
"**MOTIVATION, FLEXIBILITY,** and **TEAM SPIRIT**
are important qualities too.
and **HAVING A GOOD WORK ATTITUDE,**
makes a difference in all that you do."
"Being **HONEST** is a must,
and you need to **COOPERATE** with one another.
You have to have great **SELF-CONTROL**,
and use **SOCIAL SKILLS** with others."
"There's one more thing that you both must do
when getting and keeping a job.
You need to keep yourself **WELL-GROOMED**,
cause it's not fun to work with a slob."

(FYI: One of the biggest complaints that people have about going to work is
having to be around stinky people!)

"The choice is yours.
You get to decide what soles you end up filling.
There's a job for every personality,
as long as you are willing."

The ultimate goal of most parents is to help their children reach their highest potential possible and be the BEST they can be in ALL that they do. However, there is a catch to achieving this goal: Your child must "want it" more than you. You can teach your children all about the big list of skills and qualities, but if they are not willing, or don't see the purpose of incorporating them, the list is just a bunch of words.

I often tell parents, if you are having one of those days where you feel like you "vacuum" at parenting (a more polite way of saying, "I suck at this!") take a look at the Big List. If what you are doing causes your child to embrace and own just one or two of the skills or qualities on the Big List, you are (according to research) doing something right!

My careers research also led me to discover that according to *Forbes* magazine there are 10 abilities employers will continue to look for when considering hiring your child.[2] They are listed below in order of importance:

1. Ability to work as a team

2. Ability to make decisions and solve problems

3. Ability to plan, organize, and prioritize work

4. Ability to communicate verbally with people inside and outside an organization

5. Ability to obtain and process information

6. Ability to analyze quantitative data

7. Technical knowledge related to the job

8. Proficiency with computer software programs and other forms of digital technology

9. Ability to create and/or edit written reports

10. Ability to sell and influence others

Numbers 2 through 10 above mostly consist of academic and executive function skills, but notice the number one skill at the top of the list – ability to work as a team.

To be a good team player, a person must be able to build strong human relationship skills.

No matter how talented and hardworking your child is, if they cannot find ways to work effectively with others and share their talents to benefit the team,

---

[2] Adams, Susan, "The 10 Skills Employers Most Want in 20-Something Employees," *Forbes*, October 11, 2013, https://www.forbes.com/sites/susanadams/2013/10/11/the-10-skills-employers-most-want-in-20-something-employees/.

what value will they have in the workplace? Relationships that your child builds with others, like the one they have with you, are also dependent on TRUST and COMMUNICATION.

Teach Your Child Bounce-Back Superpowers

The world that we live in isn't always kind. When kids encounter adversity, they need to figure out how to become resilient and bounce back. Here are six BOUNCE-BACK SUPERPOWERS to keep in mind:[3]

> *Breathe*. Deep breathing helps you relax. It's one of the fastest and easiest ways to calm down and clear your head. Practice 2-4 breathing with your child:
>
>> "Take in a slow, deep breath while you count to two.
>> Breathe out and count to four.
>> Breathe in as much air as you can,
>> and breathe out even more."
>
> *Brainstorm*. Unzip your brain and pour your ideas out on paper. Keep in mind, "There's always another way."
> *Say "I Got This!"* Take that "T" out of CAN'T. Talk back to the worry that says, "I CAN'T." Incorporate the power of YET: "I can't do ______ YET!"
> *Chunk-It!* Break a big problem down into smaller pieces.
>
>> "When a problem seems really big to you,
>> and you feel like giving up,
>> break it down into smaller chunks,
>> and it won't be nearly as tough."
>
> *Ask for Help*. It's always okay to ask for help after you have tried everything you can think of to solve a problem by yourself.
> *Recharge*. Take a break when you need one.
>
>> "When you're exhausted and you can't go on,
>> look at how far you've come.
>> If you take a break and get recharged,
>> it will help you get things done."

---

[3]Cook, Julia, and Michele Borba, *I Got This! I Have Bounce Back Superpowers*, National Center for Youth Issues, Chattanooga, TN, 2024; Borba, Michele, *Thrivers: The Surprising Reasons Why Some Kids Struggle and Others Shine*, G.P. Putnam's Sons, 2021.

Dealing with Kids Who Are Not Very Nice

Kids can behave so cruelly! When another child does or says something hurtful to your kid, how do you respond appropriately when your mama or papa bear claws are about to flare?

Just recently, I heard a mom say: "This morning, I sent my kid to school beaming with pride, sporting a new haircut that he absolutely loved. Then a classmate started to tease him, making a joke about his ears being so big he could use them as antennas to communicate with Mars. Now my son is in tears, questioning his self-worth and is dreading going back to school tomorrow."

Many years ago, I came up with a phrase that seemed to help my kids through situations like this:

> **"There are people put on this planet to show the rest of us how NOT to be, and that kid is really good at his job.** I can only imagine how bad you feel inside right now. But instead of feeling bad about yourself, feel grateful. That kid just taught you the best lesson ever— how and why to be kind to others. Next time you think about saying something mean to somebody, you'll remember how it feels to be on the other side of unkind words. You never want to make another person feel like you do right now."

How to Make Friends

Friendships are very important when it comes to our emotional health! Friendships foster and teach important social skills such as active listening, empathy, cooperation, and problem-solving. Friendships may even help children succeed in academic environments.[4]

A lack of friends can have devastating effects on a child. Children who struggle with making and keeping friends often experience mental health problems such as anxiety and depression. They are also more likely to get into trouble and drop out of school. In contrast, children who have at least one really good friend can find their way through just about any challenge that life hands them.

Fortunately, there are a lot of things parents can do to help their children make and keep great friends.

- Teach your child that it's okay to be friendly and kind to everyone, but you get to decide who you truly call your friends. Also, being unkind to anyone is never okay.

---

[4]Cook, Julia, *Making Friends Is an Art, 2nd ed.*, Boys Town Press, Omaha, NE, 2020.

- Often remind your children that positives attract. The more upbeat and positive your attitude is in life . . . the more people will want to be around you and the easier it will become to make and keep friends.
- Remind them that friendships must have Trust and Communication to survive. If one or both are missing, the friendship will fail. If you are in a relationship that is struggling, ask yourself, "Is this a trust issue or a communication issue?" Then work on fixing the part that is broken.
- Teach your children how to accept and grow from feedback. Keep in mind, feedback from others is only information that can help you grow. Asking for what you need from another person is a great way to foster communication; e.g., "This time we can play what you want to play, but next time, I really want to choose what we play." Or: "I know you like to share stuff with your other friends, but next time when I tell you something important, I really need you to keep it to yourself."
- Teach, build, and model empathy whenever possible.
- Practice the Golden Rule: Treat others the way you wish to be treated.
- Teach your child that friendships and levels of friendships are fluid; they are constantly changing.
- Schedule in-person creative play dates. If in-person play is not possible, get even more creative!
- Schedule video Zoom craft-making calls for your child and a friend.
- Schedule a supervised Live Gaming Online Tournament and give out prizes to the winners.
- Have your child stream and chat about a movie with another child or group.
- Help your child find a pen pal.
- Schedule an outdoor playground date or bike ride.

You can't ever have too many friends, but having just one true friend can be a priceless gift that can help get you through life's tough situations. Don't expect all friendships to be alike, and realize they all won't last forever.

Build Academic Success

In her book *The Smartest Kids in the World*, Amanda Ripley documents many things that world-class parents are doing to foster school achievement,[5] including:

- Agreeing to the fact that a rigorous education is critical to a child's life chances.
- Allowing their children to make mistakes and even fail in a supportive environment and then get right back to work.

---

[5]Ripley, Amanda, *The Smartest Kids in the World*, Simon & Schuster Paperbacks, New York, 2013.

- Becoming an EDUCATIONAL COACH by reading to their children and talking with them about their day and news around the world.
- Understanding that parents who are most active in children's schools – PTA, staff appreciation committees, room parent, etc. – DO NOT tend to raise smarter kids. *The impact happens at home!*
- Teaching and modeling good habits.
- Giving their children autonomy.
- Becoming teachers as parents.
- Understanding the importance of academic resilience.
- Setting and enforcing predictable boundaries (physical, psychological, and emotional).
- Realizing that hard work, patience, integrity, and consequences serve a child for life.

Avoid "Peerenting"

Be your child's parent, not their peer.

Being their peer will inhibit them from developing and fostering healthy friendships with others and add conflict to the relationship you have with your child.

Kim was the mother of two kids, a 15-year-old daughter and a 10-year-old son. Her husband was a truck driver and was on the road a lot. Kim's son missed his dad immensely. Consequently, he was giving his mom a run for her money. He sported big emotions, struggled in school, had a difficult time making friends, and was frequently ending up in my office due to conflicts, control issues, and behavior.

Kim's daughter, on the other hand, was her "mini-me." They seemed to be very close and did many things together. Kim immersed herself in her daughter's social life and often told me, "My daughter is my ride or die and my best friend."

One day, while Kim's husband was working out of town, her son punched a kid on the playground and was suspended. That evening Kim was feeling understandably overwhelmed. She made the mistake of asking her daughter for parenting advice.

"What do you think my consequence for him should be this time? I'm at my wits end! Why does he have to act like this? What would you do if you were me? Any ideas?"

Kim inadvertently took her parenting throne and threw it right out the window.

The next morning, her daughter came downstairs dressed in shorty shorts and was planning to wear them to school.

"You are not wearing those shorts to school young lady!" she said. "Go upstairs and change now!"

Guess what hit the fan that morning . . .

I ended up with both Kim and her daughter crying in my office. After we talked, and they both calmed down, Kim drove her daughter to school and then came back to my office so we could talk about what happened – mom to mom.

I explained to Kim that becoming a parent comes with two roles: *Functional* and *Emotional*.

Your *Functional Role* is making sure your child has the appropriate material things they need (clothes, food, supplies, etc.) and making sure they learn how to take care of themselves physically (safety, hygiene, etc.)

Your *Emotional Role* is being your child's advocate, supporter, and ROCK through thick and thin.

When you start out as a parent, the functional role and the emotional role are equal. However, as your child grows up and matures, the functional role dissipates and the emotional role stays intact.

For example, I have an adult daughter with three kids and a very busy career. She calls me every day. I listen to her many challenges, offer support, try not to give her too much advice, and serve as her human dustpan. I am her emotional rock who will always be there for her no matter what. But I don't have to ask, "Hey, did you remember to brush your teeth today?" because my role as her functional parent has sailed.

If you try to be your child's functional parent and their peer at the same time, you'll end up paying a very uncomfortable conflict price. Think about it . . . would you want your best friend telling you how to drive, how to dress, how to stand up straight, who to hang out with, etc.?

Be your child's parent, their mentor, supporter, and a grown-up they wish to be like some day while you are functionally parenting them. Then when the time is right, and that role is complete, you can also become their friend.

This is YOUR time to sit on the parenting throne. It doesn't last long, so don't give it up too soon . . . enjoy it!"

Watch What You Share

Kids innately do all they can to make sense out of their world. If you find yourself in a stressful situation and you share too much with your children, they will take your struggle on, internalize it as their own, blame themselves, and attempt to solve your problem with an immature skill set. Chronic exposure to stress at a young age can lead to depression and anxiety and cripples your child's emotional well-being.

Here is a list of things you should NOT share with your children:

- Your personal regrets – Your child is not your counselor.
- Your financial burdens – Your child will feel guilt.
- Marital conflicts – Your child is not emotionally equipped to understand adult conflict.
- Your trauma details – Your child cannot process your brokenness.
- Negative opinions about family members – Your child will start to question their loyalty.
- Gossip – Your child will begin to copy what you normalize.
- Adult private matters – Allow your child their innocence.
- Criticism of their other parent – When you criticize their parent, you criticize half of them.
- Your insecurities – They will have enough insecurities of their own; they don't need to take on yours too.

Dealing with Separation Anxiety

Imagine how you would feel if you were dropped off in the middle of a big city in a foreign country and told, "Have a great day! I'll pick you up in six hours." This may be the way a five-year-old feels on the first day of kindergarten. Starting school is a big step for everyone involved. Dropping your child off at school and leaving them there for the first time can be both heart wrenching and extremely stressful. Fear of the unknown along with the inability to control the situation often leads to separation anxiety for both parents and their children.

As a parent, you may feel an array of emotions: **confidence** in knowing that your child is as attached to you as you are to them, **guilt** because leaving causes your child distress, and **worry** as you ask yourself: "Will my child be okay?" "How long will my child be upset?" "Will the teacher know how to comfort my child?" "Am I doing the right thing by leaving?"

There are a lot of things you can do in advance to reduce levels of separation anxiety. Here are a few tips that can help both you and your child[6]:

Visit the School Together

Take a tour of the school with your Pre-K child in the spring while school is in full session. Walk through the hallways, explore the classrooms, try out the playground,

[6]Cook, Julia, *The Lucky Button*, Boys Town Press, Omaha, Nebraska, 2025.

check out the cafeteria. Then, during the summer when you talk about starting school with your child, they will have a visual picture of what school will be like. Familiarity creates a sense of predictability and security, making the transition to school easier. Repeat this experience in the fall prior to school starting if needed.

Introduce the "Safe" People

Just like at home, school has "safe" people who will care for your child (teachers, administrators, custodians, cafeteria staff, the school nurse, etc.). Make sure your child is familiar with who to turn to if they ever feel unsafe.

Establish a Consistent Morning Routine

Routine leads to predictability, which lessens anxiety. Near the end of summer, set and enforce an appropriate evening and bedtime routine, wake-up time, and morning routine so that transition when school starts is easier and more predictable.

Practice Being Apart

Send your kids to Grandma's and Grandpa's for a weekend or two. Learning that you will always come back when you leave is a game changer.

Make Goodbyes Quick, Consistent, and Meaningful

Give your child your full attention and affection, then say goodbye quickly, even if they cry or try to convince you to stay. Prolonged and inconsistent goodbyes can increase anxiety.

Stay Calm and Positive

You might feel as much or even more separation anxiety than your child. Kids pick up on your emotions, so do your best to appear calm and positive (AKA: *Never let them see you sweat!*). Also, keep in mind that learning in every experience is hardly ever comfortable.

Comfort Items

Allow your child to carry a small token of yours or a picture of you with them to school if needed.

Get Involved

Attend open houses, family nights, PTO meetings, and consider volunteering when possible. Success at school is a team effort on all fronts. The more appropriately involved you are, the more comfortable you will become with your child's school experience. Your child will also see and feel your enthusiasm and will become more positive about being at school. On the flip side, avoid becoming overly involved. Stay in your lane. The parent role at school is crucial, but if you overextend your role and interfere with the roles of teachers and administrators, you will cause yourself a lot of stress and end up inhibiting your child's growth.

Keep in mind that every child and parent deals with separation anxiety differently. However, if intense anxiety continues after the first month, and/or interferes with daily activities, consult your pediatrician.

Teach and Model Integrity

> "Real integrity is doing the right thing knowing that nobody's going to know whether you did it or not."
>
> *–Oprah Winfrey*

When I was 11, I worked for my dad in his cutlery grinding shop on Saturdays. When my dad sharpened scissors, he'd take them apart, sharpen each blade, put them back together, and see if they were sharp enough by cutting small strands of flannel material. One day, he ran out of flannel and sent me to the mercantile three blocks away with $20 and a note for the clerk that read "10 yds. heavy flannel please." I paid with a $20 bill, and the guy mistakenly gave me back some ones and a fifty instead of a five.

"Guess what?" I told my dad when I got back. "I just got paid to buy flannel! It's my lucky day!"

My dad looked at me surprisingly and said, "You're keeping it?"

"Yep! He'll never know."

"But you will know. You'll know today, and tomorrow, and forever. You just sold out your integrity for $45. That doesn't sound so lucky to me."

With a pit in my stomach the size of Jupiter, I turned around and went back to the store to make things right.

My dad was a man of few words, high integrity, and more friends than anyone I have ever known. He never judged others. He never did stuff just to fit in. He lived by the phrase: "If you look into a mirror, and you are proud of what you see, it's a very good day." He genuinely was the "I" in integrity. I often tell kids that "integrity" is the secret ingredient that attracts friends for life.

Teaching Integrity

The big, fancy definition of integrity is "*The ability to genuinely emulate the values, morals, and beliefs that one claims to have. It is a collection of honesty, honor, courage, authenticity, respect, responsibility, and restraint."* However, when kids ask me what it means, I say, "A person of high integrity always tries to do the RIGHT thing . . . even when nobody's watching."

Basically, I think integrity is a priceless quality that some people have and ALL people need. It's a game-changing ingredient in the recipe for humanity. Integrity is also a friend-making magnet! A person who does the right thing, even when nobody else is watching, and is not judgmental of others for their choices, will never lack for friends.

Unfortunately, integrity is not innate. It must be taught and developed through both experience and example. Here are a few strategies to help foster a strong sense of integrity in the children you care for and teach.

- **Model integrity by setting a good example** – Don't make promises you cannot keep. Stay true to the commitments you set. Pay attention to your environment. Surround yourself with honest people. Stay focused on the task at hand. And finally, take responsibility for your actions. Adults who demonstrate integrity show kids firsthand that good choices lead to even greater results in life.
- **Teach the "GOODS"** – Discuss virtues, such as compassion, patience, and honesty, and use real-world examples to highlight why these virtues are so beneficial.
- **Help kids understand that healthy relationships depend on mutual trust and honest communication** – If one or both are missing, relationships fail. Having integrity means being honest and trustworthy in all situations.
- **Teach empathy** – Children who learn to recognize and understand the feelings of others have stronger social connections and demonstrate more helping behaviors.
- **Reward respectable behavior** – All kids have *"What's in it for me?"* tattooed on their foreheads. Being rewarded for positive behaviors is a great motivator and encourages kids to do similar behaviors again.
- **Explain consequences before they are needed** – When you do good things, good things happen. When you don't make the best choices, negative results and consequences happen. Never set a consequence that cannot be carried out. False threats build anxiety and confuse boundary recognition.
- **Teach, preach, and model digital citizenship** – Everyone has a technology tail. What you do, where you go, and what you say online is traceable and stays with you forever. Teach kids to always be positive and respectful when posting messages or other content. A good rule of thumb to use is *"Thumper's Rule"* from Disney's *Bambi* . . . *"If you can't say somethin' nice . . . don't say nothin' at all!"* Also, make sure kids know they can always seek the support of a caring adult if they feel threatened, bullied, blackmailed, confused, or fearful.

- **Point out that integrity can be found everywhere** – Always be on the lookout for stories, people, and events that demonstrate high integrity, and share them with your children.

Six days ago, I went to the grocery store and when the clerk gave me back some change, I noticed two twenties were stuck together. It was my lucky day! I had an opportunity to do right thing, even when no one was watching. I immediately gave the extra twenty back to the clerk. It felt good then, it feels good now, and I bet it will feel good forever.

LOOK IN THE MIRROR.
WHO DO YOU SEE?
"I JUST SEE
REGULAR ME."
AND I SEE WHO
YOU CAN BE
WHEN YOU FIND YOUR
"I" IN INTEGRITY!

Worth Remembering

- Parenting is HARD because kids don't come with instructions!
- TRUST and COMMUNICATION are the two essential ingredients needed to build a life-lasting relationship with your child. Always be appropriately honest and teach and model good communication skills.
- Know the SUCCEED NEEDS – **The Big List** of qualities and skills that will help your child with everything they need to win in the world:

Communication Skills	Listening Skills	Reading
Writing	Science	Social Studies
Math	Creative Thinking	Good Reasoning Skills
Decision-Making Skills	Problem-Solving Skills	Desire to Keep Learning
Responsibility	Being on Time	Self-Confidence
Integrity	Motivation	Flexibility
Team Spirit	Good Work Attitude	Honesty
Cooperation	Self-Control	Good Social Skills
Well-Groomed		

- Teach your child **BOUNCE-BACK SUPERPOWERS** so they can become more resilient. BREATHE, BRAINSTORM, SAY "I GOT THIS!" CHUNK IT, ASK FOR HELP, RECHARGE.
- Teach your child that it's okay to be friendly to everyone, but they get to decide who they truly call their "friends," and friendship levels are fluid and constantly changing.
- Friendships and levels of friendships are fluid and are constantly changing.
- Set and enforce predictable boundaries (physical, psychological, and emotional).
- Help your child realize that school is practice for life. Hard work, patience, integrity, and consequences will help them grow and excel.
- AVOID PEERENTING – Be your child's parent, not their peer.
- WATCH WHAT YOU SHARE – Chronic exposure to stress at a young age can lead to depression and anxiety and cripples your child's emotional well-being.
- TEACH AND MODEL INTEGRITY – A person of high integrity always tries to do the right thing . . . even when nobody's watching.

Worth Trying

TOSS THE CHICKEN

OBJECTIVE: Teach kids that devices cannot communicate as effectively as people can.

MATERIALS NEEDED: Rubber chicken or something similar that is soft to toss.

DIRECTIONS:

- Ask two people to come to the front of the room and have them stand facing each other about 10–15 ft apart.
- Give one person the chicken and ask that person to start tossing it back and forth with the other person. Toss with verbal directions 3–4 times.
- Ask the participants to start telling each other where they are planning to toss the chicken BEFORE they toss (over your head, to your right, at your knees etc.) Toss 3–4 times.
- Ask the participants to nonverbally point in the direction they plan to toss BEFORE they toss. Toss with visual directions 3–4 times.
- Have participants turn around and face the wall. Have them (without looking) explain to each other where they plan to toss the chicken BEFORE they toss it, so the other person will know where it is supposed to be coming from. Try this 1–2 times. Most of the time accuracy will be way off. If it is not, your people are standing too close together.

CONCLUSION:

1. Explain that standing face-to-face and talking is the best form of human communication possible. You learn to read a person's emotions, meaning, passion, and you hear their tone of voice, etc.

2. Explain that nonverbal communication (pointing where it will go) is still highly effective. You are in the same room, experiencing the same event at the same time, you learn to recognize emotions through body language, etc.

3. Explain that the back-to-back toss represents online communication. Oftentimes what we mean is not what others understand. Emojis cannot ever take the place of human emotions. Texting is actually a brilliant way to miscommunicate how you feel and misinterpret what other people mean.

By the way, this activity was created by a team of brilliant middle school kids who helped me create *The Techno Smart Activity and Idea Book* as a robotics project on digital citizenship.[7]

---

[7]Cook, Julia, *The Techno Smart Activity and Idea Book*, National Center for Youth Issues, Chattanooga, TN, 2015.

Worry About It! Dealing with an Overly Anxious Child

"Almost everything will work again if you unplug it for a few minutes, including you!"

–Anne Lamott

Anxiety is a basic human emotion that we all have and experience. It has a great purpose. Anxiety's job is to protect us and keep us on our toes. It helps us prepare for things that might happen so we can be ready for them. A little bit of anxiety is a true asset. It adds to our lives by bringing our strengths to the forefront, causing us to think and react at a higher level. But when our anxiety gets out of hand, it can consume our every thought and prevent us from getting things done.

When I talk to kids about anxiety, I like to use the root beer float concrete visual.

"The ice cream in this glass is everything you have going on in your life. The root beer is your anxiety. Every root beer float needs a little bit of root beer to make it taste good. We all need a little bit of anxiety. Anxiety keeps us on our toes and helps us

(Continued)

prepare for things that might happen down the road. If you have too much anxiety, that's like having too much root beer in your root beer float and before you know it, you have a big mess to deal with. Too much anxiety fills you up with worry and fear and it keeps you from doing some of the things that you need to do."[1]

Anxiety Disorder in Kids

Anxiety has become one of the biggest mental health challenges kids face today. Anxiety disorders occur when a child's worries or fears cause interference with their life for a period of six months or longer. The Cleveland Clinic reports approximately one in five of today's kids will develop an anxiety disorder prior to reaching adulthood.[2]

To effectively combat this problem, we need to become more aware of the potential causes of anxiety, be able to recognize the signs of anxiety, offer students strategies and tools to manage their anxiety more effectively, and most importantly do what we can to prevent from adding to the problem.

What Causes Kids to Become Overly Anxious?

When kids are overly anxious, they become worried and scared. This results from feeling a loss of control over their surroundings, situations, and environment. Unfortunately, some of the factors that cause increased anxiety are out of our control.

Anxiety disorders in children can be caused by many factors including:

- Genetic predisposition – Some people are naturally wired to become more anxious than others.
- Family history – Kids learn to be anxious when their parents are anxious.
- Exposure to intense trauma and/or violence – Prolonged periods of instability, unpredictability, and/or physical and emotional trauma result in experiencing a continuous uncontrollable state of feeling unsafe. Elevated and frequent FIGHT or FLIGHT responses over time cripples feelings of security and exacerbate anxiety.
- Biological anomalies – Chemical imbalance and dysregulation involving serotonin and norepinephrine levels.

---

[1]Cook, Julia, "Test Anxiety – Root Beer Floats," CookieBytes, 2025. https://cookiebytes.substack.com/p/test-anxiety-root-beer-floats.

[2]Cleveland Clinic Staff, "Anxiety in Children," Cleveland Clinic, October 2023, https://my.clevelandclinic.org/health/diseases/anxiety-in-children.

- Low socioeconomic status – Limited resources combined with societal pressures and expectations.
- Overexposure to environmental stress – Divorce, moving, targeting by a bully, etc.
- Developmental stage roadblocks – The brain is underdeveloped and cannot make sense out of the situation at hand, e.g., separation anxiety, social isolation, peer struggles.
- Overexposure to social media and video gaming – There is continuous online pressure from society to participate, achieve, perform, and conform.
- Overexposure to media events that portray anxiety or fear – You become what you watch and internalize.
- Lack of sleep – Sleep deprivation elevates cortisol and norepinephrine hormone levels in the brain, which chemically leads to high levels of anxiety, irritability, and depression. In his book *The Anxious Generation*, Jonathan Haidt identifies Sleep Deprivation as one of the four foundational harms suffered by our current phone-based generation, and he suggests it can lead to a variety of health problems beyond anxiety.[3]

Online Activity and Anxiety

Some kids endure intense peer pressure to be online overnight while they are supposed to be sleeping. Extended periods of nighttime gaming and/or online activity can sneak up on kids causing sleep deprivation induced anxiety.

Eric was a typical 12-year-old 7th grader. He had a stable family life with loving, supportive parents. In a period of about six weeks, Eric went from loving everything about going to school to becoming highly anxious, full of "What Ifs?" and afraid to leave his house. One morning, Eric's mom was standing outside my door when I got to school. She looked like she hadn't slept in days, and her face spelled out STRESSED!!! in capital letters.

"I just don't get this, Mrs. Cook. I can't figure out what's wrong with Eric. Nothing has changed or happened in our family. He's going off the deep end . . . and why?"

I asked Eric's mom if he played a lot of video games and could possibly be playing them at night as opposed to sleeping. His mom assured me that Eric was not given access to his gaming system at night.

"We have our kids charge their gaming systems in our room overnight. We've never allowed online access past 10 pm. It's a family rule."

---

[3]Haidt, Jonathan, *The Anxious Generation*, Penguin Press, New York, 2024, p. 123.

Mom did some detective work and discovered that Eric had borrowed a gaming system from his cousin, and was keeping it hidden in his room. He was setting his alarm for 1 am and gaming online with his friends every night until 6 am. He would then go back to bed and sleep until 7:30 am when his mom woke him up. When he got caught, he begged his mom to let him keep playing.

"I'm on a team mom, and I'm really good. Please don't make me quit. If I don't play, I won't have any friends at school."

Eric was sacrificing his sleep to "fit in" with his peers and ended up paying a heavy price. Six weeks of ongoing sleep deprivation had caused changes in Eric's brain chemistry. He was unable to sleep even after he no longer had access to nighttime gaming. At only 12 years of age, he became irritable, more anxious, severely depressed, and even suicidal. It ended up taking a five-day hospitalization and several weeks of both medication and therapy to get Eric's internal sleep clock back on track. I remember his mom telling me: "We almost lost our boy. I can't believe how devastating this has been. I had no idea such a simple thing could cause so much damage!"

Unfortunately, like Eric, many of the kids we teach today spend a lot of time online at night while their parents think they are sleeping. Consequently, they may be tired, irritable, anxious, and/or depressed before they even walk into our classrooms. Although we cannot control this issue, knowing what's behind it can help us become more adaptable and effective. Good teachers teach kids where they are, not where they expect them to be. Consequential sleep deprivation is not an excuse for poor behavior and performance, but it can be the reason behind it.

Recognizing Anxiety

Recognizing that a child is feeling anxious can be tricky. Although some kids may vocalize their fears, others may mask their feelings of insecurity by withdrawing, becoming inattentive, or showing big emotions. Here are a few common behaviors that an overly anxious child might display:

- Frequent reassurance and verification seeking (e.g., asking the same question repeatedly)
- Frequent stomach aches and/or headaches, dizziness, cold sweats, irregular heartbeats
- Difficulty breathing
- Loss of appetite
- Avoidance of participation in activities (e.g., presenting, demonstrating)
- Parent separation struggles
- Fear of change in daily routine

- Enhanced irritability, acting out
- Chronic avoidance of school
- A lack of focus, concentration, and motivation

We sometimes mistake anxiety in our students for other issues such as defiance, laziness, lack of motivation, or ADHD. Becoming more aware of the signs of anxiety in our kids can be key to preventing a wrong assumption.

Strategies and Tools for Managing Anxiety

Although we may not be able to prevent most of the causes of anxiety, we can teach our students a number of ways to manage it. Effective coping strategies can allow kids to gain back control of their thoughts and emotions, promote self-confidence and well-being, and build resilience.

Kids need to first understand that anxiety has a purpose. It's a normal, worthwhile emotion that everyone feels. Anxiety's job is to keep us on our toes and help us prepare for things that might happen so we will be ready if they do. Everyone feels anxious from time to time, and that's okay. But when our anxiety gets so big that it keeps us from doing what we need to do, we must figure out ways to shrink it. Here are some shrink tricks that kids might find helpful:

- Always Remember to Breathe – A few minutes of 2-4 breathing will help you relax and lower your anxiety.

> "Breathe in deep while you count to two
> Breathe out and count to four. . .
> Breathe in as much air as you can,
> And breathe out even more."[4]

- Squeeze your worries into a squishy or hold the squishy up in the air and trace the outside edge of it with your finger as you breathe deep in and out.
- Try to focus on the things you can control, not on the things you cannot. Less stuff to worry about means less anxiety.
- If something you need to do is difficult, remember the power of yet. "I can't do __________ YET." A growth mindset is kryptonite to anxiety.
- Make a list of all the things you need to get done and check them off as you do them. Crossing completed tasks off of a list feels very rewarding and encourages you to keep going.
- Talk about your worries with a grown-up you can trust. Learn who the safe people at school are so if you feel like you need help, you'll know who to ask.

---

[4]Cook, Julia, and Michele Borba, *I Got This! I Have Bounce Back Superpowers*, National Center for Youth Issues, Chattanooga, TN, 2024.

- Eat healthy foods, get plenty of sleep, and exercise. Do all you can so from the outside in so you will feel better from the inside out.
- Schedule some "ME TIME" every day. Even if it's only 10–15 minutes, take time to "unplug" from everything and do something you really enjoy (sometimes that means do NOTHING at all).
- Remember, it's okay to SAY NO to things you cannot fit in. Overscheduling creates anxiety.
- Take yourself on a mental vacation for a few minutes and visit your happy place inside your head.
- Limit screen time and balance on-screen accomplishments and celebrations with off-screen accomplishments and celebrations.
- Prepare in advance for the next day. Do as much as you can to prepare the night before (lay out clothes, get your backpack ready, etc.) so your morning will be less hectic.

What Educators Can Do to Help

Since we interact with our students on a daily basis, it puts us in a powerful position to recognize when our kids are feeling anxious, and it gives us a unique opportunity to help them work through it. Many students carry a full backpack of anxiety from home into the classroom every day. Then, when they start to worry about school stuff – grades, friendships, schedule changes, and performance – that backpack becomes even heavier.

There are many things you can do to decrease student anxiety. Here is a long list, but in no way is it too long. To me, this list is and always must remain never-ending:

- Make your classroom a comfortable place where kids feel safe enough to try, make mistakes, fix their mistakes, grow, and learn from the experience.
- Keep a calm and reassuring demeanor. Create an environment where your students feel comfortable asking questions. If they are asking the same question over and over again, know they are seeking reassurance.
- Get to know your kids so you can build on their individual strengths.
- Role play strategies to show your students how to react in certain situations. Explore both best-case scenarios and worst-case scenarios using realistic evidence.
- Allow extra time on tests when needed and/or allow kids to take their tests apart from other students.
- If a student is going to be singled out or called on for a classroom activity, let that child know a day in advance so they can feel more prepared.

- Always offer the "Phone a Friend" option when asking students to answer a question in front of their peers.
- Do all that you can to keep from bringing your own anxieties into your classroom. Anxiety can be highly contagious!
- Teach, model, and practice organization skills – BRAIN, BODY, STUFF! Organization breeds predictability, which lessens anxiety.
- View your classroom through the eyes of your students. Take some authentic time to find out what your students might be hauling around in their backpacks.
- Acknowledge and normalize your students' thoughts, feelings, and reactions. Make your kids feel seen, heard, and validated. Instead of saying "Don't worry about it." Or "I know how you feel," say "I can only imagine how ____________ you must be feeling."
- Teach with compassion and understanding for where your kids are, and where you can take them, as opposed to where they are expected to be. Your kids are ALWAYS more important than the material you are teaching them.
- Establish a predictable daily routine. – Having a clear, consistent daily schedule helps kids who are anxious feel more secure.
- Offer choices whenever possible. – Giving your students some control reduces stress, builds ownership, and enhances self-confidence (e.g., Choose between these two assignments. Pick any two math problems from each section. Design your own book report format).
- Teach with a Growth Mindset. – Always emphasize progress and effort over mastery. Mistakes are opportunities to figure out a better solution. Great people make great mistakes every day. Teach the "POWER OF YET."
- Explore the "What IFs?" with your students. By simply talking through possible scenarios, you can help kids find missing pieces to their "Making Sense Out of My World" puzzle.

Kimber was one of the most anxious kids I have ever worked with. She worried about every aspect of her being: home, school, parents, friends, relatives, etc. Her head was full of "What Ifs" and worst-case scenarios. Kimber's parents had recently separated, and she felt like her whole world was falling apart. She'd gone from a typical lighthearted nine-year-old to a kid who felt the weight of the world on her shoulders. The more I talked with Kimber, the more anxious she seemed to become. Nothing I had tried was working and, on most days, I felt like talking with her made the problem even worse.

I could only imagine what was going on inside Kimber's head. Her "What Ifs" were taking over her every thought. She had a hard time coming to school, withdrew from peers, and had a very difficult time paying attention in class.

One day on my way to work, I was thinking, "If only I had a magic recipe for all of Kimber's "What Ifs." And then, it hit me! Why not have Kimber make a recipe box that holds recipes for overcoming every worry she has? I stopped at the grocery store and bought a small plastic recipe card box and a package of recipe cards.

That morning, I asked Kimber to unzip her brain and tell me absolutely every worry she had. As she unloaded her astronomical number of worries, I feverously jotted them down on a piece of paper. Then, I had Kimber copy each worry from my paper down on the top of a recipe card. Each day, we would find time to talk through a stack of her worries.

One by one, we worked together to generate a recipe for action for each worry. Kimber wrote down her action plans on the cards and stuck them in the recipe box, which she religiously carried with her in her backpack. The deal we made was that once a card was complete, that worry could no longer take up space in her thoughts.

The "What If Box" was a game changer for Kimber. Just knowing she had a concrete plan that she could access for every "What If" allowed her to build confidence and regain control of her thoughts.

- Provide kids with a calm space to reset their thoughts when needed.
- Continually set equal expectations for all kids anxious or not. Expecting a child to be anxious will only encourage anxiety.
- "CHUNK IT." – Teach your students how to break big assignments and projects up into smaller ones. This will help your kids feel less overwhelmed and build their confidence.
- Talk about transitions and changes in routine in advance whenever possible. Also, be sure to discuss the purposes behind the changes. This will help kids prepare and ignite their "POWERS OF FLEXIBILITY" and begin to recognize that a change in routine is going to happen from time to time, and that's OK.
- Allow your students to work in pairs or small groups. Kids feel strength in numbers and learning how to work with others is a skill that will serve kids for life.
- Team up with parents, caregivers, school mental health professionals, administration, and other teachers. Collaboration, cooperation, and sharing strategies will help students feel more supported across the board.

Worth Remembering

- Anxiety is a basic human emotion that we all have and experience.
- Anxiety's purpose is to protect us and help us prepare for things that might happen so we can be ready for them.

- Anxiety disorders occur when a child's worries or fears cause interference with their life for a period of six months or longer.
- One in five of today's kids will develop an anxiety disorder prior to reaching adulthood.
- When kids are overly anxious, they become worried and scared. This results from feeling a loss of control over their surroundings, situations, and environment.
- To effectively help students who are overly anxious, we need to become more aware of the potential causes of anxiety, be able to recognize the signs of anxiety, offer students strategies and tools to manage their anxiety more effectively, and most importantly do what we can to prevent from adding to the problem.

Worth Trying

Watch the "Ring Out Your Sponge" video on `cookiebytesbyjulia.com` and then demonstrate it to your students as you relate it to anxiety and how it builds up.[5] Explain how if we don't take time to sleep, take some "me time," take time to exercise, etc. (AKA: Wring Out Our Sponge!), anxiety will keep building up until it consumes us and keeps us from doing what we need to do.

---

[5] Cook, Julia, "Ring Out Your Sponge," CookieBytes, 2025, `https://cookiebytes.substack.com/p/wring-out-your-sponge`.

11 Keeping Kids REAL with AI

"AI could be dangerous for students who lack sufficient background knowledge or critical thinking skills. If someone enters 5+3 into an AI calculator and the answer they get is 'PIG', they won't know that 'PIG' cannot be a correct answer unless they already know something about math. AI won't be a good substitute for careful study."

–J. Turner, PhD

I cannot in good conscience forget to include a chapter on AI for this book. AI advances are rapidly changing how kids learn and how we teach. AI is currently soaring in popularity, but forms of it have been around for a long time. Calculators, computer grammar checks, spell checks, and search engines are all predecessors of today's AI.

AI is both amazing and beneficial, however using it also has a downside. Kids and adults alike are becoming over-reliant on technology, which in turn is crippling self-actualization and, in some cases, leading our kids toward self-destruction. To keep this from happening, we must become more aware of AI's ever-evolving assets and deficits.

To get a more authentic look at AI in the classroom, I interviewed 54 kids ages 8–18, and over 100 teachers, school mental health professionals, and administrators. I asked them the following questions:

1. How do you use AI in the classroom?
2. Do you like or dislike AI and why?
3. Do you think using AI is good for kids?

I've included a broad representation of their responses in this chapter.

(Continued)

What AI Can Offer Educators

Humans created AI to be used as a learning tool with endless capabilities. When used appropriately, it can be a powerful asset to both educators and students.

Streamlining Administrative Tasks

Repeated and mundane tasks: attendance, documentation of incidents, newsletters and notes to parents, email drafts to staff, etc., can be done more efficiently with AI. This allows teachers more time every day to develop relationships with their students. Nearly a third of K–12 teachers say they used the technology at least weekly last school year.[1]

> "I love using AI to create my weekly newsletters for parents. It used to take me forever to make them and it was a task I always put off until the very last minute. Now I pick a differently themed template each week, enter in my info, add a few photos and send it off. I'm making myself a color copy of each one to put in a memory book for the year and saving them in a file so I can use them for future years. My parents continually comment on how much they look forward to getting their newsletters, and often ask, 'How do you have enough time to do this on top of everything else that you do?' (They don't realize it only takes me 15–20 min! SHHH!)"
>
> *–A. Bach, 2nd grade teacher*

---

[1]Shroff, Lila," The AI Takeover of Education is Just Getting Started," The Atlantic, August 12, 2025, `https://www.theatlantic.com/technology/archive/2025/08/ai-takeover-education-chatgpt/683840/.`

Creating Lesson Plans

Many teachers use AI to create and generate lesson plans, project ideas, and activities that are tailored to the specific needs of their kids as opposed to offering them a "one size fits all" traditional lesson.

> "AI helps me create worksheets for my non-traditional learners. It gives me ideas and activities for my gifted kids and helps me tailor my assignments to fit the needs of my kids who have learning disabilities. I can actually make a version for each kid if I need to. It's amazing!"
>
> *–T. Havensburg, K-12 Resource Educator*

Translating

AI can translate learning materials into multiple languages, which enhances ELL transitioning and allows teachers to support their students more effectively.

> "In my classroom, I have 6 ELL students, and I only speak English. I can take any assignment and use AI to translate it into just about any language I need to. I can also use AI as a translator to talk to my kids. I don't think I can ever go back to teaching without it."
>
> *–S. Amber, 1st Grade Teacher*

Intelligent Tutoring

AI is used for intelligent tutoring. Games can be easily created that provide practice venues and immediate feedback for customized academic skill building.

> "I have math skills practice every day for 20 minutes. My kids can log in on their tablets and play games. They are engaged and look forward to doing math, and every game they play is specific to what they need to practice. They earn rewards for following steps properly, not just for getting the right answer. What a great teaching tool!"
>
> *–M. Ortiz, 4th-5th Grade Teacher*

Tracking Performance

AI is often used to analyze student progress and performance. This helps teachers troubleshoot struggle, target resources, and customize direct instruction.

> "My students do t–heir assignments online. Based on how they do, I can tell what I need to emphasize more in class."
>
> *–H. Gaines, High School History Teacher*

Accessing Resources

AI allows educators to pull learning resources from multiple, easy-to-access sources.

> "I used to struggle getting my students to understand different chemistry concepts. How I learned them and explained them only made sense to some of my kids. AI gave me the 'HOW to say' the same thing multiple ways for different learners. It has made me a much more effective teacher."
>
> *— J. Lee, HS Chemistry Teacher*

Reducing Anxiety

AI can help reduce anxiety when we feel like we don't know enough about what we are supposed to be teaching.

> "I was told I was teaching a biology course last semester. I'm a physics teacher and I haven't even looked at a bio textbook since college. AI gave me everything I needed to brush up on the basics, and it didn't take forever to do it! I realized I knew more than I thought I did. Formerly, I was not a big fan of AI, but this experience has changed my mind significantly."
>
> *—Z. Flemming, HS Teacher*

Enhancing Critical Thinking

AI can enhance critical thinking skills and comprehension of reading/listening.

> "In my sociology class, I often use AI to create simulations of modern-day problems and have my kids work together in groups to develop solutions to those problems. This really helps my students develop their critical thinking skills."
>
> *—B. Smith, HS Teacher*

Supporting Students

AI can help prepare students for the future.

> "As a middle school/high school counselor, part of my job is to help students develop a career path that they are passionate about. I use AI to do interest and talent inventories on my kids. Using the data I collect, I then create several career simulations for each student so

they can get a better idea of what they might want to become in the future and what skills they will need to acquire."

–R. Cook, Counselor

What AI Can Do for Students

AI can also directly support students in the classroom and beyond. Here are some of the ways students can use it to improve their performance and well-being.

Emotional Support

AI can offer students 24/7 emotional support and mental health building strategies via chatbots.

> "My school counselor made us a chatbot. We named it Jelly Bean. If ever I am feeling anxious or sad, I can get online and talk to Jelly Bean and it helps me feel better."
>
>
>
> *–Angelica, 4th grade*
>
>

Source of Feedback

AI can give students one-on-one instant feedback when working on an assignment. This helps kids recognize and correct errors along the way, streamlining concept development. Children who engage in interactive dialogue with AI comprehend the stories better and learn more vocabulary, compared to those who just do the stories passively.[2]

> "I love doing math on my tablet. If I make a little mistake when I'm doing a problem, it doesn't let me keep going until I figure it out."
>
>
>
> *–Annie, 3rd grade*
>
>

Learning Engagement

AI can make learning more engaging by use of gaming.

> "I enter my spelling words into my Chromebook and AI makes cool games with them that I can play. It makes studying for my spelling test fun."
>
>
>
> *–Sebastian, 5th grade*
>
>

---

[2]Anderson, Jill, "The Impact of AI on Children's Development," Harvard Graduate School of Education, October 2, 2024, https://www.gse.harvard.edu/ideas/edcast/24/10/impact-ai-childrens-development.

Academic Support

With AI, kids can have 24/7 online academic support in starting papers:

> "I am a three-sport athlete and between practice, weight training, and going to games, I usually don't get to my homework until nine or ten at night. By that time, I am exhausted. I am taking AP classes, and the homework is really time consuming and hard. Sometimes if I can't figure out how to do something, or get a paper started, I use AI to help me. It's nice to have my own personal tutor to help me out when I get stuck."
>
> *–Channing, HS Junior*

Or:

> "I love using Math AI – Math Solver (math-gpt.ai). It helps me with homework when my teacher or websites that practices are done on don't explain the material very well."
>
> *–Joni, 7th grade*

Support for Students with Disabilities

AI helps students with disabilities by filling in the gaps.

> "I have dyslexia. I can read but it takes me forever! I used to think I was stupid and keeping up in class was next to impossible. Thanks to AI, I am now a 4.0 student. I can listen to my textbooks and required readings. I can also take tests orally online."
>
> *–Francis, HS Sophomore*

And:

> "I cannot spell, and writing is not my best subject. I love how AI edits and corrects what I type and helps me make sense on paper."
>
> *–Alexandra, 5th grade*

The Downside of AI

My grandma always said, "*Don't believe everything you hear on the radio!*" She often spoke about the scariest time in her life. On October 30, 1938, at 8 pm EST, Orson Welles and his *Mercury Theatre on the Air* broadcasted a series of realistic news bulletins that interrupted a radio dance program on CBS Radio Network. The scripts included realistic sound bites of Martians invading and destroying the planet. Some listeners (my grandmother included) inadvertently assumed that the reports were true. She remembers feeling panicked, and fleeing her home with her family, seeking refuge at the town church in fear of being killed by Martians. Mass panic subsided the next day when Orson Welles apologized and explained he was only trying to create a fun and entertaining story as a holiday offering.

AI Can Get It Wrong

In late 2023, I was goofing around with ChatGTP, and I asked it to write a biography for Julia Cook. I was surprised to find out how accomplished I was! According to AI, I received a doctorate degree in Australia! I've never even been to Australia.

Three weeks later, the current president of a state school counseling conference introduced me for the keynote as "Dr. Julia Cook." It caught me off guard and I froze. I wanted to explain the unearned title mishap to my audience immediately but feared it might make the president appear publicly uninformed, so I took a deep breath, hoped nobody was listening too closely, and started my talk.

Later that day, the president asked me "Julia, with all you have accomplished, how did you ever have time to get your doctorate in Australia?"

I winced and replied, "I don't have a doctorate . . . AI hallucinates!"

"Those who cannot remember the past are condemned to repeat it."
–George Santayana

To me, this quote speaks volumes because radio was my grandmother's AI. Note to self: Never believe everything you hear (or read!)

AI is created by input and data from many sources. An AI system's credibility is based only on the quality of data that it learns from. Consequently, AI often gives answers that are incorrect. It also can omit information by mistake, mix up facts and fiction, and make up completely fake people, events, and articles.

In the past two years, AI use in the schools has increased significantly. In 2023, Common Sense Media conducted a survey and reported that 50% of students between the ages 13–18 had never used AI tools in the classroom.[3] In September 2024, a second survey revealed that 70% of teens have used at least one type of generative AI tool.[4]

How Using AI Can Hurt Educators

As useful as AI can be to educators, there are many ways it can cause harm if relied upon too often or for too many tasks. Here are some examples.

Reduce Interaction with Students

Relying too heavily on AI activities can decrease the amount of teacher-student interaction and dialogue. This in turn compromises the building of human relationships and devalues human interaction.

> "One of my MBA students came to me and said, 'I asked AI to help me review some concepts we'd covered in class, and the AI explanation was so different from your explanation that it just confused me.'
>
> I replied, 'This is exactly why you need to reach out to me when you're confused. If you don't understand something, it's my job to explain it to you differently in a way that makes sense. AI can tell you what it knows, but it isn't as good at working with what you

[3]Center for Digital Thriving, "Teen and Young Adult Perspective on Generative AI," Hopelab, Harvard Graduate School of Education, Common Sense Media, 2024. `https://digitalthriving.gse.harvard.edu/wp-content/uploads/2024/06/Teen-and-Young-Adult-Perspectives-on-Generative-AI.pdf`.

[4]Madden, Mary, Angela Calvin, and Alexa Hasse, with support from Amanda Lenhart, "Dawn of the AI Era," Common Sense Media, 2024. `https://www.commonsensemedia.org/sites/default/files/research/report/2024-the-dawn-of-the-ai-era_final-release-for-web.pdf`.

know. AI is a tool for you to use to develop a better understanding of the material we cover in this class. If it could effectively teach this class, I wouldn't have a job."

—J. Turner, PhD, Professor of Finance

Create New Stresses

Becoming sufficient in using AI tools effectively in the classroom is both time-consuming and challenging. This puts stress on educators who already feel pressed for time and are being pressured to integrate AI into their teaching practices.

"I love teaching kids. I want my class and everything about it to be real. I am responsible for teaching history, and I want my students to know the facts, not AI's inaccurate interpretation of those facts. Besides, who has time to get good at using AI? As soon as you start to feel comfortable, it changes."

—N. Haltner, HS History Teacher

Threaten Safety

AI violates privacy and breaches security by collecting huge amounts of data.

"My district requires me to log my detailed case notes onto their school counseling platform program that many people have access to. This violates counselor-student confidentiality, puts my kids at risk, and goes against everything I believe."

—L. Louis, K-12 Professional School Counselor

Be Unreliable

AI can generate inaccurate information.

"If my kids see something online when they do an AI search, they assume it is true. This makes my job even more difficult because now I'm not only trying to teach content, I'm competing with misinformation."

—N. Gardner, Middle School Teacher

Perpetuate Biases

AI programs are susceptible to societal biases when created by biased data. Biases are also amplified when an automated system becomes a replacement for human judgment.[5]

---

[5]The University of Kansas, Center for Teaching Excellence, "Helping Students Understand the Biases in Generative AI." https://cte.ku.edu/addressing-bias-ai.

"I often use AI to pre-grade my student essays. It singles out cut-and-paste papers, flagging plagiarism. However, I no longer use it to pre-grade my ELL kids' work because insufficient language and grammar skills causes my AI program to significantly misinterpret abilities."

—G. Lee, HS Creative Writing Instructor

Create Doubt of Students' Work

AI makes it difficult for teachers to recognize authentic student effort and achievement.

"I feel like AI is compromising integrity and rupturing my ability to trust my students. I no longer give my kids take-home exams because they use misuse AI. When I assign papers, I find myself doing AI searches to rule out plagiarism. I don't have the time to verify every student response. I know some of my kids are spending more time trying to figure out how to cheat and get away with it than they are learning the material. I made the mistake last week of accusing one of my students of turning in an AI-generated opinion paper, only to find out that she did the work. Now I feel like the worst teacher on the planet!"

—A. Rasmussen, HS Civics Teacher

How Using AI Can Hurt Kids

AI also poses risks to kids if they use it too often, stunting the development of skills they need to succeed in school and life.

Reduce Critical Thinking

Overuse of AI can cause kids to lose their ability to develop individual ideas and think critically.

"Today, our teacher put us in groups and asked us to come up with a team theme for the Industrial Revolution. We could use our textbooks, but we were not allowed to ask AI or look anything up online. Everyone just sat there, and nobody knew what to do, what to say, or even how to get started. We didn't want to get it wrong, and we couldn't check online to see if we were on the right track. It made me realize how much I depend on AI to think. Maybe we shouldn't use it so much."

–Lucy, age 14

Expose Them to Misinformation

Relying on AI responses can lead students down the path of misinformation.

"In 8th grade, my social studies teacher had us do an assignment on Pocahontas using schoolai.com. One of the questions we asked AI was 'What was Pocahontas's favorite color?' Every team that asked that question ended up getting a different answer: 'Blue because her eyes were blue,' or 'Green because she loved being in nature among the trees, etc.' It made me realize that AI answers questions but the answers it gives us vary upon the day and the time asked. How can we trust AI to give us the truth?"

–Bristol, HS Freshman

Cast Doubt on Performance

AI makes it more difficult for students to prove their worth.

"I hate AI! Today my teacher accused me of using it to write a paper that was my own personal work. She can't tell the difference, so why did I spend two weeks on an assignment when I could have done what everybody else in the class did and let ChatGPT do it for me in minutes?"

–De'vone, HS Junior

Make Life Too Easy

AI weakens student resilience and perseverance.

"AI is BOMB! If ever I want to learn or understand something on a deeper level, I just ask my phone. It makes doing my homework EASY. I don't have to try hard at all anymore!"

–JT, 7th grade

Limit Creativity

As well as critical thinking skills, AI stifles creativity.

> "I don't have to be creative anymore because AI does that for me."
>
> *–Randt, HS Sophomore*

Reduce Confidence

AI promotes unlearned helplessness.

> "What I do can't even come close to what AI can do so why even try?"
>
> *–Crispin, 8th grade*

Reduce Vital Human Interaction

AI reduces meaningful student-teacher interactions.

> "AI makes teachers lazy! Today, I asked my teacher a question and he said, 'Look it up.' I had already looked it up. What I wanted was a human answer because the answer online made no sense to me."
>
> *–Brett, HS Freshman*

AI Was Created to Add to Our Lives – Not Take From It

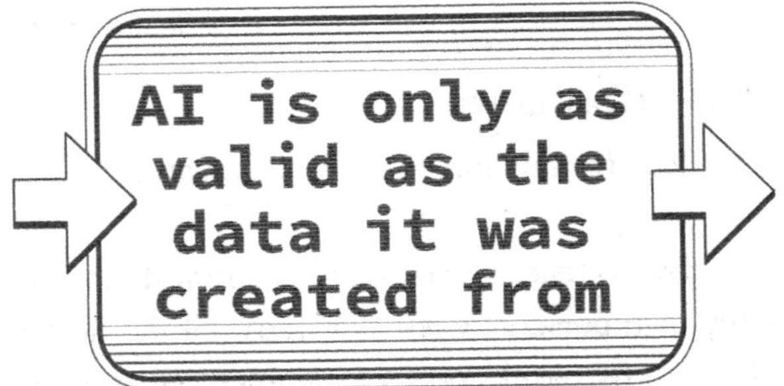

If used correctly in the classroom, AI has great potential for efficiently enhancing the learning experience of all children. It can springboard creativity, capitalize on time management, allow educators more time to be human with their kids, and provide unique, engaging, and effective learning tools foreveryone.

Misuse of AI, on the other hand, will result in having devastating effects on learning potential, self-worth, and human relationship building. According to research, constant reliance on AI will leave students without the stamina or ability to complete tasks effectively. Over-relying on AI chatbots will cripple creative thinking muscles and diminish problem-solving skills.[6]

---

[6]Saric, Ivana, "Teachers Warn AI is Impacting Students' Critical Thinking Skills," Axios, March, 2025. https://www.axios.com/2025/03/30/teachers-ai-students-critical-thinking.

Humans are the most intelligent species on the planet. We created AI and we must remain in control of what it can and will do in the future. We need to use what we have to manage what we know and use what we know to manage what we have.

College and graduate students are much more immune to the negative effects of AI than younger students who are currently building their foundations of knowledge.[7]

The key to protecting kids from the risks of AI is to teach all children to believe in themselves and trust their abilities to think critically and problem solve. Kids need to understand that AI is and always will be less amazing and less capable than they are. AI will NEVER replace human value or creativity. Creativity comes from deeply personal emotions, memories, and experiences that AI is incapable of replicating.

We all need to view AI only as a tool that we can use to help us learn and grow. Its job is and always will be to complement human intuition . . . not replace it.

Before becoming involved and interacting heavily with AI, we must equip our kids with a strong foundation built from the abilities to think critically and independently problem solve. It is important to have open-ended continuing conversations with children that explain how AI works, what it can do to help us, and how it can hurt us with misinformation. We need to teach our kids how important it is to always question AI-generated content and make sure they understand that AI truly does hallucinate!

To further protect our kids, it is crucial that we set clear boundaries for online activity, use privacy settings, and monitor their digital use. Since AI continually grows and evolves, it is imperative that we invest the time needed to stay informed of new developments so our kids can continue to positively navigate the digital world we live in.

Worth Remembering

- AI advances are rapidly changing how kids learn and how we teach.
- AI will NEVER replace human value, creativity, or critical problem-solving skills.
- Teach kids to view AI only as a tool that we can use to help us learn and grow. Its job is and always will be to complement human intuition . . . not replace it.
- The key to protecting kids from the risks of AI is to teach all children to believe in themselves and trust their own abilities to think critically and problem solve.
- Have continuing conversations with children that explain how AI works, what it can do to help us, and how it can hurt us with misinformation.

---

[7]Ibid.

- Teach kids how important it is to always question AI-generated content and make sure they understand that AI truly does hallucinate! AI is only as accurate as the data it was created from.
- AI is ever evolving. To manage it effectively, we must stay on top of what's new and continue to keep learning.

Worth Trying

THE BLIND ARTIST ACTIVITY

OBJECTIVE

Compare effectiveness of AI-generated information to human creativity and problem-solving.

MATERIALS NEEDED

- 10–12 3×5 cards, each with a unique object written on it (stingray, lighthouse, trampoline, etc.)
- Container to put the cards in
- Paper and pens for each artist to use

DIRECTIONS

1. Divide your class up into teams of five or six students.
2. Have each team pick one kid to be "the artist" and give each artist a pen and a blank sheet of art paper.
3. Ask all artists to go out into the hallway.
4. Have each team draw an object card out of the jar.
5. Explain to the teams that they will have five minutes to take turns giving clues that tell the artist how to draw the object. The clues cannot reveal any part of the object (e.g., you cannot say "Draw eyes." You must say "Draw two circles and put a dots inside of them").
6. The artist draws what he hears from his teammates and is not allowed to show what he is creating until the time is up.
7. Instruct half of the teams to use AI to generate their clues and have the other half play the game without using AI.
8. Invite the artists back in and start the activity.
9. After five minutes, stop the activity and have the artist reveal their creations.

DISCUSSION

For this activity, who was more effective at giving the artist instructions – AI or kids, and why?

12 Honey, the "Secret Sauce"

"You get more flies with honey than you do with vinegar!"

–Grandma Irene

The original form of my grandma's favorite phrase first appeared in an old Italian proverb that surfaced in 1666. Basically, it means that being *nice* is much more effective than being *not nice, and* being positive gets you a lot farther in life than being negative.

This concept seems to apply to every aspect of my life, especially when I'm working with kids. When people ask me what I do, I often say "I teach kids GPS." That stands for "great people skills." I think this description works for anyone who works with kids.

We are in the business of teaching kids great people skills (GPS for short!), and our success in this field is measured by what our kids learn, remember, and apply. In essence, the goal of a great teacher is to get kids to remember what you say!

(Continued)

Emotional Memory

When the human brain experiences an event that does not involve emotion, it creates a nonemotional memory. Nonemotional memories (fact and event recollection, skills and habits, short-term memory entries, etc.) are stored in various interconnected areas of the brain including the hippocampus, prefrontal cortex, and neocortex.

When emotions are activated during an event or experience, an emotional memory is created. Emotional memory storage is much more complex because in addition to involving the hippocampus, prefrontal cortex and neocortex, the amygdala also becomes integrated into the process.

When an emotional memory is forming, signals are immediately sent to the amygdala, which encodes, processes, and stores each emotion. At the same time, the hippocampus grabs onto the details and context of the event depending on how we are involved. Then the brain merges the information from both areas. Emotional memories are initially stored in the hippocampus and are later integrated with the rest of the brain, processed, and then permanently stored in the neocortex.

Emotional memories integrate more parts of the brain than nonemotional memories, making them much stronger and easier to recall. Learning new material is highly impacted when emotional memories become involved.

If a learning experience activates a positive emotional memory, it is sometimes called a *GLIMMER*. Glimmers make us feel good and want more.

When negative emotional memories are activated, it is often referred to as a *TRIGGER*. Triggers cause stress responses that impair cognitive functions like attention and working memory. Triggers also lead to avoidance behaviors and emotional states that are counterproductive to learning.

The Gottman Institute's research indicates that for every negative experience a person has, it takes five positive experiences to bounce back.[1] Our brains are

[1] Benson, Kyle, "The Magic Relationship Ratio, According to Science," Gottman, October 4, 2017, updated September 18, 2024, https://www.gottman.com/blog/the-magic-relationship-ratio-according-science/.

negatively biased and pay more attention to negative emotions and memories. We instinctively prioritize learning from threatening experiences to avoid future harm.

As Chip and Dan Heath state in their book *Made to Stick*, "You prioritize goals that are critical ahead of goals that are beneficial."[2]

If a student is noncompliant or avoiding an activity or assignment, always look for a possible trigger and find out what lies behind it before you react. Then, figure out a way to create at least five learning Glimmers for that student to experience.

> "I was first introduced to fractions in third grade. They made no sense to me at all. Everyone in my class could figure them out but I didn't have a clue. The harder I worked, the worse it seemed to get. One day, in 5th grade, my teacher tried to explain fractions to me with body parts (e.g. your top 1/2 is your belly button up and your bottom 1/2 is your belly button down.). Then he said, 'If I cut you up into pieces . . .' and I just froze. All I could think about was my teacher sawing off my limbs and parting me out. From that moment on, I decided I hated fractions and everything about them. To me, 'FRAC-TION' is the F Word. It literally sends me spinning. I am getting anxious right now just by writing this!"
>
> *–Annie, age 15.*

Annie was at my house last week and I had her make cookies with me. I showed her how fractions of ingredients are just like fractions in math. Then we even played around with a few fraction/cooking scenarios. Things finally started to make sense to her. Fractions were used in more of a positive light, and our cookies turned out amazing! One glimmer down . . . four to go!

The goal of teaching is to get kids to remember and apply the important things you say. When kids feel good about a learning experience, they naturally want to continue to learn more. On the other hand, when learning triggers negativity or discomfort, kids tend to repel and avoid future learning encounters.

Avoid triggers and capitalize on glimmers by finding creative ways to make your lessons positive, relatable, fun, and more engaging.

Creating Glimmers for Kids

I often ask teachers, "Would you want to be a student in your classroom?" If the answer is no, think about what you need to do to change that. Learn from your past by taking time to recall your own emotional memories.

---

[2]Heath, Chip, and Dan Heath, *Made to Stick*, Random House, New York, 2008, p. 34.

What did your great teachers do and say that helped you create glimmers?

What did your "not so great" teachers do and say to trigger you into discomfort?

If you use your unique gifts to become a "Glimmer-producing teacher" as opposed to the "Trigger instigator, you'll become much more effective with kids.

"You get more GLIMMERS with honey than you do with vinegar!"

What I See Is How I'll Act!

Whenever I talk to a large group of students, I always find it much more effective to "TALK WITH" my audience, as opposed to "TALKING AT" them, so I walk around, sit on the floor when I read, and use proximity to become more effective. "When kids are off task, I work my way toward them nonchalantly, to turn their attention.

Last year, I was talking to a large group of K–2nd graders. The students were sitting on the floor, and their teachers were sitting at the ends of each row in chairs. About halfway through my presentation, I noticed one of the 2nd graders had turned around backward and was talking with the kid behind him. I casually started to gently make my way in that direction, but a teacher quickly intercepted and softly said, "Hey there. Turn around and face the screen so you can listen to Julia Cook."

The boy looked up at her and said in a not-so-quiet voice, "Why do I have to listen? Mrs. Thompson isn't listening. She's on Facebook." Mrs. Thompson happened to be sitting to my direct left. She was so involved in scrolling, that she had missed the whole thing.

That kid had a point! Why should we expect kids to be attentive if we are not. Students are continually watching us and taking mental notes on how we act and react in every situation. Saying and expecting one thing from our students and then doing something entirely opposite makes us look ridiculous! Teachers must lead by example and demonstrate mutual respect.

- We can't expect our kids to pay attention in an assembly if we are on our phones.
- We can't expect our students to be on time if we are continually late and/or running behind.
- We can't expect our kids to be organized if our desk looks like a tornado just hit it.
- We can't expect our kids to be kind to others if we appear to be unkind.
- We can't expect our kids to love learning if we don't love teaching.

A good teacher sets expectations that they are willing to perform, which fosters trust, communication, fairness, and relationship building with their students.

Krishnakumar Ramanathan, Managing Director and Group CEO of S & S Power, defines the **3 C's** of successful management as: **C**reating new products or services, **C**ontinuing excellence in operations, and **C**hanging in tune with the times.[3]

It's easy to compare this model to successful classroom management. We are the boss. Our students are the employees. The **3 C's** of success in school include:

- **C**reating innovative assignments and products
- **C**ontinuing excellence in operations by setting and modeling clear expectations for both kids and teachers
- **C**ontinuing to change in tune with our kids

"The life you live is the lesson you teach!"

–Author unknown.

---

[3]Ramanathan, Krishnakumar, "The 3Cs of Management – Simplified!" Linked In, June, 2024, `https://www.linkedin.com/pulse/3cs-management-simplified-krishnakumar-ramanathan-lvmmf/`.

Leave It at the Door

Earlier in this book, I told you the story of TJ and his backpack full of rocks. The "leave it at the door" concept applies not only to kids, it also applies to us. We all have a backpack full of rocks that we haul around every single day. The battle scars that we have earned playing the game of "LIFE" shape who we are and who we will become.

When I do a kid talk, I have found that the more I actively involve my audience in the presentation, the more they seem to get out of it. I typically ask four to five kids to come up at different times throughout the event and help me with hands-on visuals. So often after the kids have gone back to class, I have had staff ask me questions like, "How on earth did you know to pick that kid? That was just what he needed."

Or "She lost her father last month to suicide and this is the first time I have seen her smile."

And "That child struggles in class and has a really hard time with behavior, yet he sat in this talk for a full hour, and you made him feel like a rock star! How did you know to pick him?"

I always reply with a question: "Has that kid had to deal with trauma?" Usually, the answer is yes.

The phrase *"It takes one to know one"* pretty much sums up what I am getting at here. What we have endured and continue to confront shapes who we are and who we will become. The rocks in our own backpack give us empathy and an authentic understanding of how some kids see their world. They don't offer an excuse for behaviors. Instead, they teach us to genuinely understand the reasons behind those behaviors.

Our rocks weigh us down with hurt, anger, regret, sadness, and many other negatives. But carrying that backpack makes us stronger both inside and out. The next time you walk into your building, take a deep breath, remove your backpack full of rocks, set it outside of the doorway and walk inside. Your rocks will be waiting for you at the end of the day, but inside of your school walls, you get to do what you love most of all . . . you get to work with kids.

Helping a Grieving Student

> "Grief is like a snowflake. Sometimes it comes one flake at a
> time, other times it comes like a blizzard. It always melts, but
> it always comes back."[4]

---

[4]Cook, Julia, *Grief Is Like a Snowflake*, National Center for Youth Issues, Chattanooga, TN, 2011.

One month into my first year of school counseling, I had a second-grade boy whose 3-year-old brother went down for a nap and never woke up. Three weeks later, one of my 3rd-grade girls watched her 35-year-old father die of an aneurism in her kitchen. Two broken kids . . . one green school counselor . . . what a mess!

I was under the assumption that I was the perfect person to effectively help both of my students migrate through their grief process. My assumption was incorrect. I started meeting with each child individually. My goal was to have them create a memory book over a 6–8 week period of time in honor of their loved one.

Everything I did with my 2nd grader seemed to work amazingly well. For Christmas that year, he gave his mom the priceless gift that he had created. Three years ago, I received a letter in mail from that kid.

Dear Mrs. Cook –

I wanted to let you know how much you mean to me. Eighteen years ago, you helped me get through the worst time of my life. Now I would love you to be a part of the best time in my life. Please come to my wedding. Your invite is enclosed.

The first time I met with my 3rd grade student ended up being the last. Every time she saw me in the hall or felt like I might approach her in any way, she ran. My face inadvertently became a painful reminder of that day in her kitchen. Consequently, I could never be the person she needed or wanted to talk to no matter how hard I tried. I referred her to a grief group called Rainbow Kids. It was a much more effective fit for both her and her family.

Grief is like a snowflake. Everybody does it differently. Grieving is unique for every person, and there is no wrong or right way to feel.

Because of limited life experiences, kids grieve much differently than adults. Here are a few tips to help support a grieving student in your classroom:

- Know your role and limitations – Work with your school counselor, social worker, and parents to promote an effective support system for your student. Communication is key!
- If a child asks you a question that you don't know how to answer, or feel uncomfortable answering, it's always okay to say, "I don't know, but I will help you find out who to ask."
- Make your classroom feel warm, safe, familiar, and supportive.
- Maintain a normal routine – This provides children with a sense of stability and security and reassures them that the adults in their lives will continue to take care of them.
- Expect many emotions – Grieving children will experience a variety of emotions including sadness, anger, guilt, confusion, jealousy, and even happiness. Expect emotions to come and go quickly. A child may be crying one moment and playing the next.
- Encourage play – Play is a normal and healthy output for children.
- Allow choices – Following a death, a child's world will feel unpredictable. Offering choices will help promote a healthy grief experience by allowing the child to regain a sense of situational control.

Keep in mind that grief is not only caused by death. Grief is a natural human response to any significant loss. Grieving is what we do to adapt to the changes we endure after losing someone or something we care about.

They say, *"Time heals all wounds."* I think time allows us to collect glimmers that we can stick onto the outside edges of our grief. We never get over the loss. The pain we feel remains constant. But glimmers experienced over time collectively wrap our grief and buffer its intensity. This in turn makes migrating thru the grief a bit more doable.

Use "And" Not "But"

AND and BUT are two words that are easily interchangeable in conversation. However, using AND is much more impactful. AND adds to the validity of the situation, while BUT takes away from that validity. For example: One of your students is having a difficult time, and has to be escorted out of your classroom to calm down. He returns just before class is over. What do you say to him when he comes back?

"Today was a tough day for you in here, BUT tomorrow is a brand new day. I can't wait to see what you do with it."

or

"Today was a tough day for you in here, AND tomorrow is a brand new day. I can't wait to see what you do with it."

By using BUT, you are discrediting the actions that lead up to being removed from class as if it wasn't that big of a deal. This conveys to your student that his undesirable behavior didn't really matter one way or the other.

However, if you use AND, you are recognizing the undesirable behavior and increasing your student's accountability for that behavior as opposed to discrediting it. Yet, you are still encouraging positive future behavior.

Here's another example:

"I can't believe you wrecked my new car, but I still love you."

VS

"I can't believe you wrecked my new car, and I still love you."

Say NO to But . . . instead use AND!

Attitude Is Everything!

"Life is 10% of what happens to me and 90% how I react to it."

–Charles Swindoll

Attitude is a small word that impacts life in a huge way. Teaching a child to change a negative attitude into a positive one can be a difficult process. Here are a few tips:

- Help your students understand how negativity affects them.
- Teach your kids that they CAN be in control of how they feel. Attitude is and always will be a choice!
- Teach your students how to actively look for the positives in every situation. *"Every cloud has a silver lining if you can figure where to look."*
- Show your kids ways to figure out what is causing their negative attitude. Finding the cause of negativity is much more effective than focusing on positive thoughts.
- Teach kids to recognize the differences between internal negativity and external negativity.
- Highly discourage negative self-talk.

- Create a positive environment in your classroom.
- Continually remind your students that although they cannot control some things, they do have control over how they choose to feel about everything.

Worth Remembering

- The goal of a great teacher is to get kids to remember what you say!
- Emotional memories integrate more parts of the brain than nonemotional memories, making them much stronger and easy to recall.
- Our brains are negatively biased and pay more attention to negative emotions and memories. We instinctively prioritize learning from threatening experiences to avoid future harm.
- It takes five positive emotional memories (glimmers) to counteract just one negative emotional memory (trigger).
- Glimmers make us feel good and want to learn more.
- Triggers cause stress responses that impair attention and working memory. Triggers also lead to avoidance behaviors and emotional states that are counterproductive to learning.
- Teachers must lead by example and demonstrate mutual respect.

Worth Trying

- If a student is noncompliant or avoiding an activity or assignment, always look for a possible trigger and find out what lies behind it before you react.
- Talk WITH your students rather than AT them. Walk around, sit on the floor when you read, and use proximity to become more effective.
- Leave your "backpack full of rocks" at the door when you enter your classroom. Try it for one day! Then another. Then another!
- Say NO to But . . . instead use AND!

Afterword

So far, my life has been filled with "I never thought I'd(s)." I never thought I'd become a teacher, a school counselor, an author, a presenter, a keynoter, and especially a brand name. But most of all, I never EVER thought I'd become the author of a thick book with lots of words!

My dad used to say, "Juli, you have more BS in your head than anyone I know. If you can figure out a way to put it down on paper, you might just have something."

He also said, "Keep throwing your BS up against this wall. As long as it sticks, you'll be okay. But if it starts to run back down the wall, you'd better get out of the way, or your feet will start to stink."

This book is full of my BS, but in this case the BS stands for my "BEST STUFF." I threw it into this book and I hope it sticks to you in a good way!

If you are just beginning your educator journey, getting ready to retire, or somewhere in the middle, my hope is that you can see yourself in these pages and find something in them that makes your job more enjoyable and a little bit easier.

We've all been in classes and sat through professional development sessions that made us think, "Why am I sitting in here? Why do we have to read this . . . it doesn't even apply to me! This is a total waste of my time!"

I want *Teach Kids, Not Content* to be a "Get To" read book, not a "Have To" read assignment. Its purpose is to add to your already way too busy life as opposed to taking from it.

My first team leader was an amazing educator. She had so many creative teaching ideas and was always willing to share them with me. She once told me, "An idea can only become a great idea if others can use what you give them, put their own spin on it, and make it their own. Ideas don't teach your class, Julia, you do!"

This book is full of ideas for you to do just that. Thumb through the pages and think about the things that are WORTH REMEMBERING. Use this book as a reference, a handy tool, and a place where you can look for credible teaching strategies that really work with kids.

Each day as you walk into your classroom, keep in mind, you get to work with the future! How cool is that? Think about why you chose to go into teaching in the first place. Who and what made you believe that you have what it takes to make a positive difference with kids? Maybe you've experienced situations similar to the ones you've just finished reading about. Maybe you will encounter some of them in the future. Now you have a better game plan for what to do, how to respond, and how to prevent. Teaching is a "learn by doing" profession, and there are so many "doers" out there that you can learn from.

Today, I met a doer! I was working on this conclusion in a busy airport and started talking to the lady next to me. She was a beautiful, retired teacher who I'm sure left huge footprints to fill when she left.

"I never had a problem with kids because I always listened to the WHY. Students fought hard to get into my class because they knew I would fight to keep them in there. They called me the "Excuse Eliminator." If they didn't come to school, I'd drive to their houses and pick them up. If they swore too much, I'd give them other words to use instead. If they needed clothes or food, I found a way to provide for them.

In return, I expected great things from my students. I believed in my kids and robbed them of every excuse possible to not believe in themselves. We started where they were and away we went. I tried for them, so they tried for me. I'd turn them. Once they caught a glimpse of who they could become in my eyes, they grew. I lost only a few in 39 years, but I have no regrets. I got to be a teacher."

I could have listened to her for hours. The glimmer in her eyes as she talked about her career made me realize even more that every experience we endure makes us the educators we are today. Everything we do in class validates (or invalidates) our worth as a teacher, a leader, and most importantly, a caretaker of young minds.

Teaching is not easy, especially as our world and the expectations we face continue to change rapidly. If you are feeling overwhelmed, worn out, or discouraged, you are not alone! If it seems like the energy in your classroom is working against you, there are real-world solutions. If at the end of the day, you feel that you are not enough, there is a way to change that, one kid, one idea, one class, one day at a time. It's a big pie. You cannot eat it all in one sitting, but you can figure out ways to savor every bite.

Do you ever look in the mirror and think, "This job is NOT what I signed up for!"? Has your "difference-making joy" seemed to disappear? It's hard to go to work when you don't like your job. It's even more difficult to pretend you do in front of a kid. If you honestly do not enjoy teaching kids, you need to get out. But before you do that, take a look at the WORTH TRYING ideas in this book and give them a shot. Look back over the "Tricks of the Trade" chapter and try out a few tricks. You've worked long and hard to get where you are. Our kids can't afford to lose any more great teachers. You are worth the TRY and so are our kids.

The idea behind writing *Teach Kids, Not Content* was to offer positive glimmers of insight along with a few constructive methods designed to ignite your creativity as an educator. I want this book to reinvigorate your passion for teaching and offer unique ways to help you tackle your daily challenges more effectively. There's no way to overestimate how important it is to enter a child's view of the world! The kids are THE most important thing. Without them, we don't have a purpose. We should never let the content we teach, test scores, or demands placed on us by administration and parents become more important than the kids we are teaching!

The next time you start to feel discouraged, confused, or irritated by a student's action, think about TJ and the backpack full of rocks that he struggled to carry around daily. He was angry at the world and was fighting to survive the only way he knew how. Once TJ and I took time to communicate, he realized that *he* was a priority to me, regardless of how he acted. Once he started to feel safe when he walked into my classroom, we started building trust. From that trust and communication came a valuable relationship, something that TJ had never experienced at school before. Through that relationship grew self-worth, and confidence that TJ had never felt before. When TJ felt seen, heard, and validated, things changed for the better . . . including his math scores!

For me, this experience helped me understand that every behavior is a result of an unmet need. If we deal with the behavior, we put a Band-Aid on the problem that will continue to be ripped off, replaced, and reapplied. If we take time to figure out how to fill the unmet need, the problem resolves itself.

Remember the importance of shifting to a "Get-To" mindset and away from a "Have-To" mindset. Using that language every day in the classroom changes the way children experience projects and quizzes and tests. A "Get-To" is an opportunity. A "Have-To" is an order. We naturally use more of our talents on things we get to do vs things we are told we have to do.

Stop teaching content to kids. Instead, teach kids content! When it comes to effective teaching, the relationships that you build with your students heavily outweigh the subject knowledge that you possess. When you ask people about their favorite teachers of all time, chances are they will tell you about the teachers who made them feel like they mattered, not the teachers who claimed to know the most about their subject area. They'll remember the most from teachers who magically connected learning with purpose, action, and emotion.

Experiences you endure and situations that arise in your future will continually impact and shape your effectiveness as a teacher, so let them bring out the best in you!

Remind yourself that it's a privilege to share a classroom with a kid like Philly who didn't let anything stop him, even a permanent crushing loss of hope. James, whose wake-up call in his senior year inspires me to this day. Shawn, who shared his honest opinion as to why he hated school. Veronica, who showed me how to spell GRIT during high school. Mrs. Jones, who learned about Growth Mindset, Reason, Inspiration, and Talk from her student Kylar.

When we open our hearts and our minds, we get to learn more from kids than they ever learn from us.

With each passing day, it's becoming increasingly clear that we are all in this world of education together. It's not just about kids, educators, parents, and administrators, it's about everybody.

When our kids move on from school, they need to know how to work, interact, and live in the world with everybody! There are so many moving parts that it's hard to focus on any one concept at a time. In order to get the "BIG picture," we, just like our kids, sometimes need to have a solid encounter with the ITs to thoroughly gain an understanding:

SEE "IT."
HEAR "IT."
FEEL "IT."
DO "IT."
DEMONSTRATE "IT" TO SOMEBODY ELSE.
and
RELATE "IT" TO SOMETHING WE ALREADY KNOW.

Using concrete visuals is a great way to make this process fun and much more doable.

Teach Kids, Not Content, includes 10 of my favorite concrete visuals. For more, visit `cookiebytesbyjulia.com`, the Tier 1 behavior prevention website that inspired the creation of this book.

Always remember, teaching is like playing the game of volleyball. The kids are the ball, the parents are the passers, the peers are the hitters, and *you* are the setter.

There's no way you can control how kids come to you. There's no way to take charge of what happens after kids leave your presence. But if you can continually "better the ball," if that kid is better off because of time spent with you, that's a win and that's enough for today.

Focus your energy on the things that are in your control and channel your effectiveness. Don't let the uncontrollables in life get in your way.

Kids aren't the only ones continually missing pieces from the "Making Sense Out of My World" puzzle. Each of us needs to be appropriately honest with ourselves as to where we used to be, where we are right now, and where we think we'll end up.

Whenever you are faced with a challenge, use your own "Bounce-Back Superpowers" from Chapter 9 to figure things out.

- Breathe.
- Brainstorm.
- Say, "I got this!"
- Ask for Help.
- Recharge.

This book starts out with a story about my kindergarten teacher, Mrs. Hansen, who showed me how to believe in myself at the age of 5. She was a teacher who saw my gifts, encouraged me to share them, and rewarded me with appreciation for doing so. She was a teacher who made a positive difference in my life.

Now it's your turn. Remember your "Mrs. Hansen." Become the difference maker like the teachers who made the difference to you!

Keep in mind, there is truth in the phrase, "use it or lose it." According to the Harvard Business Review, we forget 75% of what we learn within six days unless we use it.[1] If you like something you've read in this book, don't wait too long to try it out on your kids. But if time gets away from you, and life takes over, that idea and a few others will always be waiting for you in the pages of the big thick book with many words.

My life has taken me places I'd never thought I would go.

None of this would have happened if kids couldn't see themselves in my books and parents, educators, and mental health professionals didn't see value in my content.

"Read a book, teach a life skill" is my bucket list dream that I could not have achieved without all of you. And for that, I say thank you for seeing value in my BS.

[1] Glaveski, Steve, "Where Companies Go Wrong With Learning and Development," *Harvard Business Review*, October 2, 2019, https://hbr.org/2019/10/where-companies-go-wrong-with-learning-and-development.

Acknowledgments

A special thanks to Dale Crawford for drawing what's inside my head, Rich Prosch for keeping my ADHD brain organized and on track, Wiley Publishing for encouraging me to write this big thick book with lots of words, Robert Rabon for helping me recognize my purpose, and most of all, my best friend and husband, Carter Cook, for being my ROCK!

About the Author

Julia Cook is nationally recognized as an award-winning children's book author and parenting expert, and her books have been referenced in such publications as *Parent's Magazine, The New Yorker, Green Child Magazine, The Huffington Post, The Chicago Tribune,* Yahoo.com, and BabyZone.com. She has also been featured on CNN's HLN News and several large metropolitan networks.

Julia was born and raised in Salt Lake City, where she became actively involved in teaching children how to ski, an experience that led to a love of teaching in general. Julia now lives in Northern Utah. Her Master's degree is in Elementary School Counseling. While serving as a professional school counselor, Julia often used children's books to enhance her classroom lessons.

Julia has presented in thousands of schools across the country and abroad, and she regularly speaks at national education and counseling conferences. She has published over 100 children's books with a wide range of characters and social development topics. Her books showcase her innate ability to enter the world-view of children, who can then use her storybooks to grow. Julia gives children both the "what to say" and the "how to say it."

The goal behind Cook's work is to actively involve young people in fun, memorable stories and teach them to become lifelong problem solvers who possess great people skills. Inspiration for her books comes from working with children and carefully listening to counselors, parents, and teachers, in order to stay on top of the ever-changing needs in the classroom and at home.

In her spare time, Julia enjoys spending time with her husband, family, and puppies.